OUR BIBLE

OUR BIBLE

J. McKEE ADAMS, Ph.D.

Late Professor of Biblical Introduction
The Southern Baptist Theological Seminary
Louisville, Kentucky

BROADMAN PRESS
NASHVILLE, TENNESSEE

ABOUT THE AUTHOR

Dr. J. McKee Adams was born in North Carolina in 1886. He was a graduate of Wake Forest College and held the Th.M. and Ph.D degrees from the Southern Baptist Theological Seminary. For 24 years he was a professor in the Southern Baptist Seminary. He was an authority on biblical archeology. For twenty years he was head of the Department of Biblical Introduction of the Seminary. His book *Biblical Backgrounds* was widely used as a textbook on the geography and customs of the Holy Land. He was one of the best loved teachers of his generation. He died in his office at the Seminary on September 17, 1945, and is buried in Cave Hill Cemetery in Louisville.

Copyright, 1937
The Sunday School Board
of the
Southern Baptist Convention
Nashville, Tennessee

Printed in the United States of America
5.25MH543

TO

DOCTOR I. J. VAN NESS

WHO SERVED THE BAPTIST SUNDAY SCHOOL BOARD

WITH HONOR AND DISTINCTION

FOR THIRTY-FIVE YEARS, SEVENTEEN AS EDITORIAL

SECRETARY AND EIGHTEEN AS EXECUTIVE SECRETARY,

THIS BOOK IS AFFECTIONATELY DEDICATED.

CONTENTS

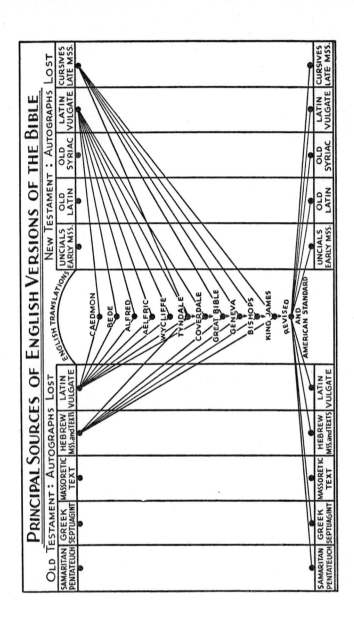

PRINCIPAL SOURCES OF ENGLISH VERSIONS OF THE BIBLE

OLD TESTAMENT : AUTOGRAPHS LOST

New TESTAMENT : AUTOGRAPHS LOST

| SAMARITAN PENTATEUCH | GREEK SEPTUAGINT | MASSORETIC TEXT | HEBREW MSS. and TEXTS | LATIN VULGATE | | UNCIALS EARLY MSS. | OLD LATIN | OLD SYRIAC | LATIN VULGATE | CURSIVES LATE MSS. |

ENGLISH TRANSLATIONS

CAEDMON
BEDE
ALFRED
AELFRIC
WYCLIFFE
TYNDALE
COVERDALE
GREAT BIBLE
GENEVA
BISHOPS
KING JAMES
REVISED
AND
AMERICAN STANDARD

| SAMARITAN PENTATEUCH | GREEK SEPTUAGINT | MASSORETIC TEXT | HEBREW MSS. and TEXTS | LATIN VULGATE | | UNCIALS EARLY MSS. | OLD LATIN | OLD SYRIAC | LATIN VULGATE | CURSIVES LATE MSS. |

INTRODUCTION

As we begin these outline studies in the origin and development of the English Bible, announcement is made by the American Bible Society that the number of languages in which the Bible has been printed, either in whole or in part, is now over one thousand. These languages include not only the principal tongues of the leading people of the world, but also some of the dialects of remote tribes who never touch the main stream of the world's life. The chief explanation of this great translation movement is found of course in the modern missionary enterprise. The success of missionary endeavor in taking the gospel to every part of the human race has reproduced the conditions that underlay the expansion of early Christianity when it became necessary for all evangelized peoples to have the records of the kingdom of God in their own languages. Consequently, practically every nation and tribe may now hear, read, and study the wondrous things of God in their own speech. This is evidently a part of the divine purpose. The gospel is intended for all men and must be made available for them in ways that they can understand. The achievements of the century now closing show that the Bible, the one Book for all mankind, quickly establishes itself as a common possession wherever given, and begins to fulfil its great mission as the savor of life unto life, a guide and a lamp to the stumbling feet of the nations. It is one of the wonders of its worldwide application that the Bible is at home in America, Palestine, England, Africa, Syria, and Japan.

The first book to issue from a printing press was a Latin Bible. Though the exact date is not known, it was during the period 1450-56. In the latter part of the fifteenth century it is estimated that 144 editions of the Latin Bible were printed in various parts of

Europe, while in the sixteenth century the number of editions increased to 438 until now. The Scriptures are available in over 1,000 languages. It is agreed that the annual output of Bibles and portions of the Bible now exceeds 30,000,000 copies. We should remember, however, that the chief glory of the Bible is not found in the number of its editions or copies, but in its unfailing mission as a beacon light pointing to God, and as an untiring teacher showing the children of men how to reach him through Christ.

The greatest single factor in the development of life among English-speaking people has been the Bible. Its unique position in the life of our forefathers has been attended by unique results. The whole of our cultural, political, social, and religious history has been powerfully influenced by the English Bible. It is our great heritage. To cherish the Bible in the modern generation of youth is to show in part an appreciation of the heroic struggles of the pioneers in English Bible translation who sought to make the Word of God available to their generation. But the Bible deserves to be studied for its own sake; its message needs to be understood; its claims repeated and acknowledged, and its one mission fulfilled, that is, to reveal the unceasing activity of God in seeking to bring to the sons of men the abounding life in Christ. In simplest terms the Bible is the record of God's acts in redeeming love. We can never understand the plan of the ages apart from the Book of ages, nor the increasing purpose of God apart from the leading of the Spirit of truth in making his Word known. If we continue to move in the sphere and spirit of the Bible we are assured at once that we will continue in broadness of outlook, fervent in love, evangelistic and missionary in our program of sharing with others the things of Christ, and generous in our support of the Lord's work.

If the present volume contributes in any way to a fuller appreciation of the significance of the Bible in Christian life and work, the author will be grateful.

J. McKee Adams

Louisville, Kentucky

DIRECTIONS FOR THE TEACHING AND THE STUDY OF THIS BOOK FOR CREDIT

I. Directions for the Teacher

1. Ten class periods of forty-five minutes each, or the equivalent, are required for the completion of this book for credit.

2. The teacher of the class is given an award on the book if he requests it.

3. The teacher shall give a written examination covering the subject matter in the textbook, and the student shall make a minimum grade of 70 per cent. The examination may take the form of assigned work to be done between the class sessions, or as a final examination at the end of the course.

Exception: All who attend all of the class sessions; who read the book through by the close of the course; and who, in the judgment of the teacher, do the classwork satisfactorily may be exempted from taking the examination.

4. In the Graded Training Union Study Course, a seal for Course IV, The Bible, is granted to young people or adults for the completion of this book.

Sunday school credit may be elected by the pupil. Application for Sunday school awards should be sent to the state Sunday school department and for Training Union awards to the state Training Union department. These departments will provide the forms for these applications. They should be made in duplicate and both copies sent.

II. Directions for the Student

1. In Classwork

(1) The pupil must attend at least six of the ten forty-five minute periods to be entitled to take the class examination.

(2) The pupil must certify that the textbook has been read. (In rare cases where pupils may find it impracticable to read the book before the completion of the classwork, the teacher may accept a promise to read the book carefully within the next two weeks.)

(3) The pupil must take a written examination, making a minimum grade of 70 per cent. (All who attend all of the class sessions; who read the book through by the close of the course; and who, in the judgment of the teacher, do satisfactory classwork may be exempted from taking the examination.)

2. In Individual Study by Correspondence

Those who for any reason wish to study the book without the guidance of a teacher will use one of the following methods:

(1) Write answers to the questions printed in the book, or

(2) Write a development of the chapter outlines.

If the second method is used, the student will study the book and then with the open book write a development of the chapter outlines.

In either case the student must read the book through.

Students may find profit in studying the text together, but where awards are requested, individual papers are required. Carbon copies or duplicates in any form cannot be accepted.

All written work done by such students on books for Sunday school credit should be sent to the state Sunday school secretary. All of such work done on books for Training Union credit should be sent to the state Training Union secretary.

III. Interchange of Credits and Awards on Comparable Subjects

One award, either for Training Union or Sunday school, is granted for completing this book.

J. E. LAMBDIN
Secretary and Editor,
Training Union Department,
Baptist Sunday School Board

C. AUBREY HEARN
Director of the Study Course

REVELATION

OUTLINE

INTRODUCTORY

1. DEFINITION OF THE TERM

II. THE METHOD OF REVELATION
    1. God Is Able to Communicate with Man
    2. Man Is Able to Receive God's Communications

III. THE OBJECT OF REVELATION
    1. God Is a Personal Being
    2. God Is the Almighty Being
    3. God Is the Saviour of the World

IV. THE MEASURE OF REVELATION

V. THE PLANE OF REVELATION

VI. THE RECORD OF REVELATION

REVELATION

INTRODUCTORY

The student's approach to the study of the Bible should be along the line of its historical development, beginning with the first steps and continuing until it stands before him as a finished product. The first requirement of Bible study is the recognition of divine activity in human experience making for an orderly and progressive unfolding of the will of God to men. The earlier phase of that process took place in the experiences of the chosen people of Israel and is recorded in the Old Testament, while the latter falls within the New Testament period heading up in Jesus and the apostles. The first books of the Bible, the five books of Moses, were written one thousand four hundred years before the dawn of the Christian era; the last portions, the writings of the apostle John, are placed at the close of the first Christian century. Here is a period of approximately fifteen hundred years in which historic development of the Scriptures was taking place, the full growth being reached when all of the several parts both of the Old and New Testaments were brought together into one volume, the Bible. As will be pointed out later, there is no great difficulty in marking the stages of this orderly growth, but the fact here emphasized is that the Bible must be studied in relation to historic order, *the product of the Spirit of God working in and through human experience.*[1]

---

[1]Over against this view of the origin of the Bible is the Mohammedan tradition regarding their sacred book, the *Koran.* For centuries Mohammedan leaders debated whether the *Koran* was created or uncreated. The theory that prevailed was that there was a "sending down" of parts through a period of about twenty-three years, until the whole of the *Koran* was in the hands of the prophet. The parts sent down, however, were not the products of Mohammed's thinking nor had anything to do with human thought, but had previously existed on the "perfectly preserved table in heaven."

Our purpose in thus stressing the divine and human
elements in the making of the Bible is to place the Word
of God at the center of human experience where it belongs. It was written neither for angels nor by angels,
but for men and by men under the direction and influence of the Spirit. This is the proper approach to the
Bible. It is reasonable and understandable because it
falls within the range of life. The Bible was never intended as an object of worship, rather was it given to
show men *how* and *whom* to worship, to lead them to
reach up for divine light and fellowship. It is not within
itself the revelation of God to men, but the witness of
his self-revelation which began in the Old Testament
and reached its perfect expression in Jesus in the New
Testament. No truer estimate was ever put on the
Scriptures than that uttered by Jesus: "Ye search the
scriptures, because ye think that in them ye have eternal life; and these are they which bear witness of me;
and ye will not come to me, that ye may have life."[2]
The Scriptures, then, stand as the permanent and final
record of how God has made himself known to the world
in Christ in redeeming love and grace. In accepting this
view we thereby exclude all other books as secondary in
interest and importance. All the light that the world
needs in order to find God is reflected in the Bible. Regarded from any viewpoint, it is undergirded throughout
with the purpose of God to save the world. Redeeming
love is a part of every page of the Bible story, just as
the water-mark is a part of the writing paper, and can
never be removed without destroying that in which it
is embedded.

Now when we define the Bible as the final record of
God's self-revelation, we definitely characterize it as
falling within the realm of religion. It is a religious
book. Here one finds the spiritual biography of the
human race. No good can possibly come from making
unreasonable demands on the Scriptures or by claiming

---

[2] John 5: 39-40. The American Standard Version has been used in Scripture
quotations throughout the book.

for the Bible final authority in spheres where it has no prime concern. The student should never call in the Bible to settle the numerous questions of scientific research, whether in the realm of biology, astronomy, physics, medicine, philosophy, or geology. Its vocabulary is not scientific, but spiritual, ethical, moral, and social. Its chief concern is with relations between God and men. It is the authority on religious experience and in this sphere will bear the most searching study and investigation. This is not to say that biblical statements regarding matters of scientific interest are not true or are not important, but simply that all such interests are secondary to the principal theme of the Bible which relates to God in saving grace and mercy. Here we may stand in full confidence, claiming for the Scriptures the final word regarding tne quest of God for men, and how redemption was finally achieved through his self-revelation in Christ.

It is now in order to ask, What is meant by *revealing activity* of God? What is *self-revelation* or *self-disclosure?* But perhaps more fundamental for us at this point is the simple question, What is *revelation?* And, finally, in what manner is the Bible the record of God's activity in revealing himself?

I. DEFINITION OF THE TERM

The word "revelation" was brought over into the English language from the Latin. Its root meaning is "to unveil" or "to uncover" so that what was hidden was now made known. In turn the Latin word expresses the term originally used in the Greek New Testament which means "drawing back the veil," a vivid conception of drawing apart the curtains in order that the audience may follow the action of the play. One book in the New Testament is called The Revelation, thus indicating that its contents have to do with the unveiling of the future, or giving a preview of the events which will occur in the future. Accordingly, when we state that

God is engaged in revealing activity, we mean that he is drawing back the curtain from that which is hidden; his self-revelation is the act of making himself known, the disclosure of his nature and of his purposes with regard to men and the course of the world. Those are the elementary ideas in the word. When we attempt to define the term so as to include the biblical conception of revelation, we meet with difficulty. As expressed in the fine words of Principal Fairbairn: "Revelation can only concern what is so above nature as to be beyond the power of man to *discover* or of nature to *disclose;* in other words, it must relate to God, proceed from Him, and be concerned with Him." From which it is clear that we are concerned only with the activity of God in making himself known. But any activity of God in revealing, in the nature of the case, must be on the order of that which is above the natural, hence supernatural. With this in mind let us attempt another statement. Revelation is the supernatural act or divine process in which God gives to the human messenger or writer glimpses of himself, his will, and his truth. No writer in the Bible undertakes to explain how revelation takes place; the fact is simply stated that the origin of all "unveiling" of the divine nature and purpose is God. It is therefore God communicating with men the truth about himself for a special purpose or end.

II. The Method of Revelation

Though there is no biblical statement as to the method of revelation, we are not left wholly in the darkness regarding certain conditions under which it must have taken place. We know that man is not the source of revelation nor is it a development of any resources within him. God reveals, man receives, and all that man has ever received has been given to him. The act of revelation has therefore at least two aspects, the divine and the human; the first being the source, and the second the goal. Now two conditions are necessary in order that revealing activity might occur.

1. *God Is Able to Communicate with Man*

The Christian view of God is that he is the supreme personal Being directing all of the affairs of the world in keeping with his will and purpose. He is therefore purposeful and responsible in all divine activity. The world is not ruled by blind chance or natural law, but by the will of God. Being interested in the affairs of men, he takes part in all events and determines their outcome in keeping with his purpose of grace. In other words, God is not detached from men and the world. He is able to speak and to be understood. Any other view would be fatal to the very idea of the existence of God and of man in a world of order and purpose.

2. *Man Is Able to Receive God's Communications*

This is a necessary condition of revelation and is based primarily on the spiritual nature of man who was created in the image of God. We understand that "the image of God" refers to no outward form answering to the physical characteristics of man, but that he is perfect in his spiritual and moral nature, in his intelligence and will. God is spirit. Man, created in the image of God, shares with his Maker likeness in kind, though not in degree, of spirit, moral qualities, intelligence, and possession of will. The receiving end of a wireless system of communication is perfectly in tune with the broadcasting point. When God flashes out the revelations of himself, man is the only creature in all the world who is constituted to understand him. Of equal importance is the fact that man is not only capable of understanding the divine message but that he is actually made with the desire to "listen in," to feel after God, to reach up and to follow the gleam. It is this ability to hear and this inclination to reach up that mark him as the highest order of creation and as a being of the God kind.

III. The Object of Revelation

As expressed in the Bible idea of revelation, God is engaged in the great process of making *himself known.* All revelation comes from him and is concerned with him. While nature cannot reveal God nor man discover him unaided, God unveils himself to the vision of the mind and heart of man. In a real sense revelation is the result of fellowship with God. There is an increasing understanding of truths about God that results from this spiritual contact which is essentially revelation in the Christian sense. Man can never know God fully; while he can be partially known, the perfection of his Being holds out the eternal hope of enlarged vision. It is important that we name here certain steps in man's growing conception of God, the steps that are intended to lead on forever to higher things.

1. God is a personal Being, perfect in all of his nature of holiness, goodness, purity, love, truth, mercy, and grace. Jesus revealed God as the loving, Heavenly Father.

2. God is the Almighty Being. By this is meant that he is self-sufficient, Sovereign over all the created universe which came from him. All power belongs to him, its source and author. God rules the world and directs its end.

3. God is the Saviour of the world seeking always to bring deliverance to sinful men through the offer of salvation in Jesus.

IV. The Measure of Revelation

In a true sense the capacity of man is a measure of God's revelation. If we are to come to knowledge of God in experiences of life, it must be one of growth and increase. In the epistle to the Hebrews there is a fine statement of this fact: "God, having of old time spoken unto the fathers in the prophets by divers portions and in divers manners, hath at the end of these days spoken unto us in his Son."[3] That means that revelation has been piecemeal and at separated seasons because of the limitations of man. He could not receive it all at one time nor can he now take in fully everything that God is desirous of telling him. In other words, the process continues while God unfolds himself to man, new truth being added to the old, fuller light to that which is in part, and more knowledge to that which has been appropriated by the believers. It is true that we shall never know all about God; deeper understanding awaits the searching heart.

V. The Plane of Revelation

In the nature of the case, if revelation is to come to man it must reach him where he is. Man is a creature of time and sense, subject to limitations of space. He moves from one point to another on the plane of history, adapting himself to his environment or changing it for the development of his life and character. This is the place where God meets him, where he reveals himself in saving grace. It is the glory of the Christian idea of revelation that, while men are stumbling, searching, and crying out for God, feeling for him as gropers in darkness, God stoops, descends into the midst of life for saving ends. The supreme revelation of God to the world was made in his Son. In the earthly career of Jesus we have the full and final answer to every thought of God concerning man. It was on the plane of historical experience that his life was lived, where he labored and died as "the Lamb of God, that taketh away the sin of the world."[4] It is on the plane of historical experience that man understands the need of that revelation and receives it.

[3]Heb. 1: 1-2.
[4]John 1:29.

VI. The Record of Revelation

Finally, the record of revelation is the Bible. The Bible tells us all that we know about God, every fact that we know about Jesus. But everything that it says has been made known to men through the working of the Spirit. The Bible was not created, but grew as the enlightened heart and mind of man received the truth. Man did not always understand everything that the Spirit revealed, but here faith entered to assist him in accepting and believing. We regard the Book as setting forth the history of man's redemption in clearest terms which all can understand. It meets all religious needs of the human heart and life, and in the realm of religion it is sufficient, trustworthy, final, and authoritative.

This does not mean that God is no longer speaking to men, or that revealing activity has ceased. If that were true, the whole of Christian experience would of necessity be on a declining rather than an ascending scale. The truth already revealed and partially known ever expands as the thoughts and purposes of men are broadened to receive and to follow its fuller meaning. One of the functions of the Holy Spirit is to illumine the minds of men for a larger reception of the meaning of salvation and service in Christ. "He shall glorify me: for he shall take of mine, and shall declare it unto you."[5]

That is a continuous process in the present life of the Christian; nor is there any statement that it will end in the world to come. The great Saviour can never be fully known; the best that we can do is to strive to lay hold on the outer garment of the mysteries of his Person, his sufferings, and his kingdom as they shine out in the Bible. In this manner we must approach the Book of love and life in sincerest effort to know him, the fellowship of his sufferings, and the purpose of his grace through us for others.

[5] John 16: 14.

QUESTIONS FOR REVIEW

1. What is the first requirement of Bible study?

2. What is meant by the divine and human elements in the making of the Bible?

3. With what aspect of human life is the Bible concerned?

4. Define revelation. What is meant by self-revelation?

5. Is revelation a natural or supernatural process?

6. What are the two conditions under which revelation must take place?

7. What is the object of revelation? Name three steps in man's growing conception of this object.

8. In what sense is man's capacity a measure of God's revelation? Discuss.

9. Why is revelation confined to the plane of history?

10. Discuss the Bible as the record of revelation.

INSPIRATION

OUTLINE

INTRODUCTORY

I. DEFINITION OF THE TERM "INSPIRATION"

II. THE BIBLICAL CONCEPTION OF INSPIRATION
   1. 2 Timothy 3:16
   2. 2 Peter 1:19-21

III. MODERN THEORIES OF INSPIRATION
   1. Plenary Verbal Theory
   2. Naturalistic Theory
   3. The Mechanical Theory
   4. The Dynamical Theory

IV. THE RESULTS OF INSPIRATION
   1. Unity of the Bible
      (1) The beginning
      (2) The progress of redeeming love
      (3) The consummation of the kingdom of God
   2. Authority
   3. Sufficiency
   4. The Influence of the Bible
   5. The Finality of the Bible

INSPIRATION

INTRODUCTORY

In our study up to this point we have been looking at the Bible as the record of God's self-revealing activity on the plane of history. We have sought to justify the claim that all the knowledge that men have of God has come from him. The biblical records clearly show that it was the purpose of God to reveal himself to men, and that his self-revelation was in part dependent on the ability and preparation of men to receive it. In the fine phrase of Dr. John R. Sampey, there is accordingly an "upward slope from the Old Testament to the New" as the nature and purpose of God are gradually understood. It follows of course that the end of this upward movement was reached in Christ, the revelation of the Father, full of grace and truth.

We must now make another inquiry which has to do with the method God employed in producing and preserving the revelation thus given. This introduces us to the general subject of inspiration as applied to the Bible. While revelation and inspiration are closely related, the distinction here made between the two should be clearly held in mind: revelation is concerned with the truth received; inspiration has to do with the method of its communication and preservation. If we hold in mind that it is simply the distinction between *what* has been revealed and *how* it was revealed, we will steer clear of many difficulties. Or, if the student prefers, he may think of the two questions of revelation and inspiration as aspects of the same thing. In both cases it is God at work revealing himself, the former being concerned with the knowledge given, and the latter the manner in which it was made known. In other words, How does

God communicate with men? What is the fundamental condition under which knowledge of God is imparted? And, finally, in what sense is this imparted knowledge reliable or trustworthy? All of these questions deal with the nature and result of inspiration and to these we turn for discussion.

I. DEFINITION OF THE TERM "INSPIRATION"

The student will probably be surprised to learn, first of all, that the words "inspire," "inspiration," and "inspirational" are not biblical terms. They have come into the English language from the Latin. As we shall see when we come to study how the Scriptures first came into the hands of our forefathers, these words are derived from the Latin Bible. While used in the early English Bibles, they have gradually found a decreasing place in our recent versions.[1] In all probability the English Bibles of the future will omit them altogether though, in the religious sense, we will continue to speak of "inspire" and "inspiration." It is clear, of course, that we are here dealing merely with the *words* that are used to express inspiration, and not with the *fact* of inspiration. Whenever the words are employed they describe an external power or influence producing in human experience results beyond the ordinary or natural.

No attempt to define inspiration has hitherto proved acceptable to all students of the Bible. As a working basis, however, it is fitting that we come to agreement as to the general idea. While the following statement is not intended as a complete definition, the facts included are beyond question: inspiration is the result of the divine power working on, in, or through the prophets, apostles, and writers which enabled them to deliver or to record in a trustworthy manner the truth received in revelation. It follows that the divine control thus exer-

---

[1] They are confined now to the following: The noun in Authorized Version, Job 32 :8 ; 2 Tim. 3 :16; and the verb in the American Standard Version, 2 Tim. 3 :16.

cised in the production of the message rendered the result
divinely credible and authoritative.

II. THE BIBLICAL CONCEPTION OF INSPIRATION

There is no statement in either the Old Testament or
the New that may be regarded as a formal definition of
inspiration. No writer thought it necessary to attempt
to explain it in whole or in part. On the other hand,
though there is no formal statement, the *fact* of inspiration is expressed everywhere throughout the Bible. The
following selected statements give the biblical background: "God, having of old time spoken unto the fathers in the prophets";[2] "Thus shalt thou say unto the
children of Israel, Jehovah, the God of your fathers, the
God of Abraham, the God of Isaac, and the God of
Jacob, hath sent me unto you";[3] "Now Jehovah had revealed unto Samuel";[4] "According to the word of
Jehovah which the man of God proclaimed";[5] "Hear
the word of Jehovah";[6] "And I heard the voice of the
Lord, saying, Whom shall I send, and who will go for
us? Then I said, Here am I; send me."[7] "And thou
shalt say unto them, Thus saith Jehovah of hosts, the
God of Israel";[8] "The word of Jehovah came unto me";[9]
"The word of God came unto John the son of Zacha-
rias";[10] "Called me through his grace, to reveal his son
in me, that I might preach him among the Gentiles";[11]
"Men spake from God, being moved by the Holy
Spirit";[12] "Write therefore the things which thou saw-
est, and the things which are, and the things which shall
come to pass hereafter."[13]

From the Scripture quotations given above, one is impressed with the fact that the written or spoken word is
always represented as coming from God and as belonging
to him, though delivered by or through a messenger.

[2]Heb. 1:1.
[3]Ex. 3:15.
[4]1 Sam. 9:15.
[5]2 Kings 23:16.
[6]Isa. 1:10.
[7]Isa. 6:8.
[8]Jer. 25:27.
[9]Ezek. 7:1.
[10]Luke 3:2.
[11]Gal. 1:15-16.
[12]2 Peter 1:21.
[13]Rev. 1:19.

Indeed, the Old Testament statements claiming divine authority either directly or indirectly number approximately four thousand. To these might be added numerous passages from the New Testament. But nowhere is there any statement that professes to define *how* God inspired men, or to explain in what manner the Spirit acted on the messenger or writer. There are two New Testament passages, however, that are of great importance in their relation to inspiration and to these we turn for brief consideration.

1. *2 Timothy 3:16*, "Every scripture *inspired of God* is also profitable for teaching, for reproof, for correction, for instruction which is in righteousness." This passage states nothing with regard to *how* the Scripture is inspired, but sets forth the fact that every scripture, or all Scripture, that is inspired is also profitable. The word here translated "inspired" really means "God-breathed." We understand that this statement refers to the whole body of the Old Testament as God-breathed with the result that it carries with it divine authority in all matters of faith and conduct. The same statement applies to the New Testament and with the same force. Here then the *result* of inspiration is in view.

2. *2 Peter 1:19-21*, "And we have the word of prophecy made more sure; whereunto ye do well that ye take heed, as unto a lamp shining in a dark place, until the day dawn, and the day-star arise in your hearts: knowing this first, that no prophecy of scripture is of private interpretation. For no prophecy ever came by the will of man: but men spake from God, being moved by the Holy Spirit." This passage, though it does not go into detail, is our main biblical statement as to *how* inspiration took place. It clearly states the fact that men were under the influence and control of the Spirit as they spoke and wrote. And that is the fundamental thing in inspiration. But the word translated "moved" has a significant meaning; it expresses the double idea of *taking up and bearing along*. The idea

here is that the speaker or writer was under the controlling power of the Holy Spirit, and that the Spirit was thus speaking through him the Word of God. Now if we ask the details of that process, there is no answer. No biblical writer goes into any explanation. It is simply a statement of fact. That it is a true statement, however, and that it is overwhelmingly supported, will appear later when we set forth the results of inspiration.

III. MODERN THEORIES OF INSPIRATION

As we have already seen, biblical writers never undertake to explain their inspiration. They are content with the simple statement that God is speaking to and through them to men. On this question there is no doubt. They also know that the Holy Spirit is the controlling power in and authoritative source of communicated truth and, further, that they are under his leading and control. Beyond that fact and that conviction they never care to go. It is well that they left it there for, after all, there remain unexplored realms of spiritual activity into which the mind of man can never fully enter. This is one of them. But that which was denied to the mind *to explain* was granted in richest measure to the life *to experience*. In a word, *how* God can inspire is overshadowed by the blessed realization that he *does*.

The modern world, however, has not been content to leave inspiration unexplained, but has rushed in with various views which seek to set forth how God acted on, in, and through men in the production of the Scriptures. The following are some of the theories advanced. They are mentioned here not because of their merit or demerit, but to bring out more clearly the main point of biblical emphasis.

1. *Plenary Verbal Theory*

The two words here used, "plenary" (full) and "verbal" (word), set forth the main points in the theory. In this view of the Bible every word employed was chosen by the writer and at the same time chosen by the Spirit. Though the Holy Spirit is the author of the Scriptures, the human agent was never disregarded. Yet, the activity of the Spirit was so uppermost in the writers that their words became the words of God. Every word, in a sense, is from man, and every word is from God. The distinction always is that God is the source and man the agent of expression. On this view, furthermore, is based the doctrine of the infallibility of the Scriptures, meaning, of course, that there is no error of any kind in the Bible. Every statement of Scripture, of whatever nature, is held infallibly true.

This, of course, refers to the Scriptures as they were originally written, and not to the various translations.

2. *Naturalistic Theory*

Simply expressed, this theory of inspiration holds that all men are divinely inspired because God dwells in all men. On the basis of creation, man partakes of the nature of God, of divine light. There is a spark of divinity in all. Whatever differences there are as to the degree of inspiration, these may be explained on the basis of natural and mental capacities, or spiritual powers. In a word, inspiration varies according to the degree of human faculties and capacities. This view would include Shakespeare, Emerson, Carlyle, as well as Isaiah, John, and Paul. The Bible offers this view no support in its main contention.

3. *The Mechanical Theory*

Under this view of inspiration the human aspect is reduced to a minimum. The writer becomes simply a machine without any choice or responsibility. In general the mechanical theory regards the writers of the several books of the Old and New Testaments simply as secretaries or stenographers, penmen whose work was to receive dictation and to put it down without change.

4. *The Dynamical Theory*

According to the dynamical theory the writers of the Scriptures were moved by the Holy Spirit who directed them through their natural and spiritual faculties. As over against the verbal theory, this view holds that only the thought in the Scriptures was inspired; the form that the thought took depended on the writer. Furthermore, there is no error in the content of the Scripture, though the words are those of the scribes. The indwelling power of the Spirit guaranteed that the message would be divine and infallible, though the writer would be free to express the message in the terms of his own mental, spiritual, and cultural advantages.

IV. THE RESULTS OF INSPIRATION

From this brief review of the four principal theories of inspiration, it is clear that the matter is not perfectly explained. In all probability we will never understand fully the process by which the Holy Spirit produced through men the sacred writings, the Bible. On the other hand, full understanding is not required. We know that the writers themselves were not concerned about the *theories* of inspiration, but laid great stress on the *results* of inspiration. *How* the Spirit expressed the will of God to men, was one thing; *what was the will of God* thus expressed, was another. And it is to the latter that the writer always turned rather than to the former. In following them, therefore, we seek not here to explain the process of inspiration; we accept it as a fact that needs no formal theory to make it real. The fruits or results of inspiration are the final and convincing arguments as to its reality. To some of these results we turn for a brief discussion.

1. *Unity of the Bible*

Among the genuine marks of the inspiration of the Bible none is more readily seen than its unity. By this is meant its inner connectedness both as a whole and in its several parts. It is not an artificial unity that one must read into it, but a natural and essential unity that binds it together. This fact becomes more marvelous when we think of the many books that make up the Bible, the many writers who appear in the production of these books, and the centuries that separate the earliest writings from the latest. The unifying bond is seen throughout just as the watermark on paper. While there are many phases of this unity, the whole Book is concerned with one thing—the record of God's redemptive work; it is his story written on the plane of human affairs. We may regard it for the present as having three distinct features, as follows:

(1) *The beginning.*—It provides us with a picture of the spiritual state of man in the early dawn of history when Adam and Eve enjoyed unbroken fellowship with God. This was followed by an awful collapse, a break in fellowship, when sin entered into human life. Out of this condition of man's fall and helplessness to regain his lost estate, God holds out the promise of a future victory which would restore man to fellowship with his Creator and redeem him from his sin.

(2) *The progress of redeeming love.*—The progressive unfolding of the divine plan and purpose to save is recounted through all the pages of the Old Testament from the earliest days to the latest. Patriarchs, lawgivers, priests, prophets, and teachers make mention of the purpose of God as revealed both to individuals and the nation. The great figure on whom this development centers is the Messiah. His mission in the world is solely for salvation. The whole history of the Hebrew people, from the time of Abraham to the advent of Jesus, is unified in the person and mission of the Messiah. God promised Abraham in Ur of the Chaldees that in him and his seed the nations of the earth would be blessed. That promise was fulfilled with the coming of Jesus in Bethlehem of Judea two thousand years later.

(3) *The consummation of the kingdom of God.*—The Bible unites in all of its parts and in the onward sweep

of its victorious Messiah to proclaim the day of triumph for righteousness when the reign of peace, justice, goodness, and truth shall have no end. This is not only the outlook in the Old Testament; in the New Testament also the onward movement of the Christian forces has for its inspiration and its goal the complete triumph of the risen Lord and his church. Thus the great victory foretold in the early chapters of *Genesis* is flashed on the screen once again in the triumph of Christ in the *Revelation*. The element of time in this redemptive plan and purpose is considerable, but there are no breaks in the unity of the records. God reigns and triumphs through his grace in Christ now and evermore.

When one looks out from the pages of the Old Testament, he expects the New Testament to swing into view to complete the picture; when one considers the old promises in the old days, when God spoke to the people through the prophets, he seeks for the record of their fulfilment in the new days; as he follows the trail of redeeming love and mercy through the centuries, he longs for the goal; and, when all the records center on the promise of his *coming*, the heart wants to know when he *arrived*. The record of the Book is complete and in perfect harmony from beginning to end. The whole story is there, unified throughout and no part missing. The Old Covenant and the New become one in Christ. Whatever is wrapped up or foreshadowed or foretold in the Old Testament, must come to the surface in the New Testament; the New Testament folds back on the Old. Both are *complementary* and *supplementary;* and both stand as the perfect records of the divine Author who succeeded in writing only *one story*, though expressing his words through many writers, through many centuries.

2. *Authority*

The Scriptures carry definite authority as the Word of God. This is also a genuine mark of their inspiration. It is not authority relating to any and every sphere, but only to the field of religion. It is not authority based on external force or compulsion, or exercised by taskmaster or autocrat, but rather an inward and spiritual authority that answers to and explains all the claims of the Christian experience. Fundamentally, its authority is the constraint of love and loyalty to God in all relations. In matters of Christian faith, it is the final word; here one finds the revealed will of God on all doctrines beyond which there can be no appeal. In matters of practice, both as relating to individual conduct and the accomplishment of the organized work of the church, it is authoritative. Here the requirements are perfectly clear regarding ordinances, worship, and work.

3. Sufficiency

By this is meant that the Bible gives all the light that is needed to show the way to God, to explain the conditions and the nature of salvation, to guide in the least details of Christian living, and to support in all the experiences through which the Christian passes. Herein we find the vital testimony of saints of the ages to the goodness and constancy of God; the counsel of the Spirit in the face of difficulties and questions; the lamp unto struggling souls in darkness, and the beacon of perennial hope and good cheer to the faithful. There is no circumstance that might befall the trusting heart but is fully answered by the divine Book. Its sufficiency applies to all men in all needs. To the unsaved it brings the word of conviction, caution, and urgency, calling to repentance and faith. In the hands of the Holy Spirit the truth herein set forth becomes the sufficient means for the transformation of the believing repentant into the likeness of Christ. This Word lives and works, and will remain the supreme record of God's purpose and desire to save unto the uttermost all who seek and call upon him.

4. *The Influence of the Bible*

The Book that has won and held the first place in human affection and reverence wherever introduced thus proves itself divinely inspired. It is the one Book for all mankind, universal in its appeal, in its application of truth, and in its spirit. It constitutes the permanent foundation on which the highest type of civilization has been built. The Bible has been the greatest single factor in the cultural, political, social, and religious progress of all English-speaking people, and is proving to be the same savor of life unto life among other peoples. As an intellectual and social influence it stands unique. In its great teachings on the value of individuals—men, women, and children; in its emphasis on the home and church; in its positive direction to care for the needy, to relieve suffering, and to lift the burdens of men; in its leading to effect peace and brotherhood among the nations, and its ideal of close co-operation and association; in its call to giving and sharing, serving and blessing, in all of these influences the Bible has no peer and no rival. Its positive influence on the history of the world marks it divine, and this shall continue to be its glory and its providential mission.

5. *The Finality of the Bible*

"There is but one Book, the Bible," said Scott to his servant. He was right. There will never be another. We are not dealing here with religious literature alone, for other religions have their sacred books and writings to which their followers ascribe light and leading. *But they have never led to God,* and never will. They lack, and their deficiency is their doom. The Bible not only claims to be the Word of God, but that claim has been verified in the experiences of untold millions through all the ages who have found him by following its light. Here, then, we find the supreme record of his self-revelation, nor will God ever say more to the world than he has already said and herein recorded. For the Bible is not only the divine witness of his messages to the patriarchs and prophets, but it also stands as the living witness of his final revelation in Christ. It could never be more than that, and it cannot be less. This does not mean that God has nothing else to say to the world, nothing else to reveal, for, in a sense, he has merely begun; but that which he will say and reveal in the future will be the outgrowth of the truth in Jesus. Through the illumination of the Holy Spirit, the understanding of the ever-expanding truth in Christ, we must always be in the process of laying hold but never mastering the full significance of his revelation. The Bible, accordingly, takes its place in Christian experience to lead on and to encourage in the ceaseless quest for light and life.

QUESTIONS FOR REVIEW

1. What is meant by the "upward slope from the Old Testament to the New"?

2. Distinguish between revelation and inspiration.

3. What is the origin of the word "inspiration"? "Inspire"? Is the use of such words increasing or decreasing? Why?

4. How would you define inspiration?

5. Quote some passages from the Old Testament giving the biblical background of inspiration.

6. What is the meaning of 2 Timothy 3: 16?

7. Explain 2 Peter 1:19-20.

8. Name four modern theories of inspiration, giving their chief characteristics.

9. Discuss the unity of the Bible.

10. In what sense is the Bible to be understood as authoritative? Sufficient? Final?

THE CANON OF SCRIPTURE

OUTLINE

THE CANON OF SCRIPTURE

INTRODUCTORY

In the preceding chapter we have been concerned with the content of revelation which was given by the Holy Spirit through the writers of the Old and New Testaments. The record of that revelation from the earliest to the latest days has been preserved for us in the sacred Scriptures of the Hebrews, on the one hand, and in the sacred writings of the first century Christians, on the other. In view of the fact that both groups of writings were inspired by the same Author, deal with the same subject, and are mutually dependent, we now regard them as one, and to the whole body of these records, consisting of thirty-nine books of the Old Testament and twenty-seven books of the New Testament, we apply the term "Bible."[1] But if we regard the Bible as divided into two divisions, the Old and New Testaments, we may go a step further in definition. To the several books that form the Old Testament we may apply the term the "Canon of the Old Testament," and to the body of New Testament books, the "Canon of the New Testament."[2]

---

[1]The term "Bible" has a very interesting history. It comes from the Greek word *"Biblus"* which means the bark of the papyrus plant, but was later applied to the pith from which writing paper was made. In process of time it was applied to the writings themselves, consisting of rolls, scrolls, or sheets of paper, hence a *Book.* The plural of the Greek word is *"Biblia,"* meaning books. The Greek plural was brought over into the Latin but was later regarded as a singular noun, *"Biblia,"* meaning the Book, from which is derived our English word "Bible." Since the Bible, the one Book, consists of many smaller books, the development is readily understood.

[2]The word "Canon" is derived from the Scriptures. The original meaning of the term in Greek usage was a *rod,* straight line, or rule used by carpenters and masons. The word gradually came to suggest anything that was of the nature of a measurement or standard, a norm, or requirement. In applying the term to the Bible, or to the divisions of the Old and New Testament, we mean that the Scriptures are to be accepted as the standard rule of faith and practice. It is, accordingly, the authoritative standard by which human thought and conduct are judged or measured.

Again, if we combine the two groups we may use the same term in a more embracing sense and speak of the *Canon of the Scriptures*, that is, the whole Bible. While we may omit further discussion of this last statement regarding the *Canon of Scriptures*, since the two parts go to form the whole, we must examine more carefully the divisions themselves in an effort to know, *first*, the original languages in which they were written; *secondly*, the various books composing each division; *thirdly*, how the old texts were preserved through the centuries; and, *finally*, how and when they were brought together to constitute the Old Testament and the New Testament and thus our Bible. Since the Old Testament precedes the New both in point of time and preparation, we turn to it first for examination.

I. THE OLD TESTAMENT

The body of sacred literature that we now call the Old Testament is derived entirely from the inspired writings of the Hebrew people. Though they were not known as the Old Testament by the people of Israel, they were regarded with deepest reverence, and acknowledged as the words of God in all relations both of the individual and the nation. As will be seen later, some of these old writings were produced at a very early period in the history of Israel, while other portions were written very late. But under the guidance of the Spirit they were finally brought together as the "oracles of God," "the holy scriptures" which were to remain the spiritual and religious possession of the Hebrews for all time. They hold that position for Jews everywhere today for, while these writings have become the Old Testament of the Christian Bible, they are also cherished by the Jews as the revelations of God to their fathers. It will be of interest here, accordingly, to describe these writings in order to trace the process by which they have been brought to us.

1. *Language of the Old Testament*

While the English Old Testament gives no indication of its foreign origin, the student must remember that originally it was produced by the Hebrew people in their own language. So far as we know, every book in the sacred collection of Hebrew Scriptures was written by a Hebrew. With the exception of a few passages, every verse in the Old Testament is in the Hebrew language.[3] The Hebrew is not a dead language. It is now spoken by Jews in various parts of the world being used extensively in orthodox synagogue services. Hebrew is also being revived as the speech of the Jews who are returning to Palestine in connection with the movement of Zionism. It is a language rich in ethical, moral, social, and spiritual terms. In form it is composed of twenty-two letters which are called consonants, or radicals, four of which have the value of vowels.

The materials used for these writings were of various kinds. While all prepared material was very expensive, paper, which was made from the papyrus plant, was the most common. It was also the most perishable except in Egypt where the atmosphere was dry and desert sand preserved the buried treasures. The material used was parchment or vellum. Both of these were made from animal skins and used extensively by the Hebrew scribes for the sacred writings. All writings were done with ink and pen, or quills. These skins were cut in the required shape and put together in lengthwise fashion and rolled up. One may get the correct idea of a Hebrew scroll or roll from the visit of Jesus to the Synagogue at Nazareth.[4] Accordingly, they were not placed be-

---

[3]The exceptions referred to are found in Daniel 2:4 to 7:28; Ezra 4: 8 to 6:18; 7:12-26; and Jeremiah 10:11. These are in the Aramaic language which is closely related to the Hebrew. After the return of the exiles from Babylon, Aramaic became the language of the Hebrews and, in the time of Jesus, the apostles, and Hebrew Christians, was their mother tongue. Hebrew was the language of Israel, generally speaking, from the time of the conquest in Canaan to the Exile, while Aramaic gradually became the language of Palestine from the restoration until the destruction of Jerusalem in A.D. 70.

[4]Luke 4:17, 20. Compare Jeremiah 36:2, 23, 28; Revelation 6:14.

tween two covers as a great book, but each roll stood to itself as the scroll of Isaiah, the scroll of Joshua, the scroll of Nehemiah, and so on.

2. *Divisions of the Old Testament*

These written records or sacred Scriptures of the Hebrews were grouped into three main divisions, suggesting probably the three steps by which they were finally brought together into one body or, as we now say, the Old Testament, though that term was not then in use. It is not necessary here to go into the details of these divisions nor into the question as to the periods in which these steps were taken. We must mention the divisions, however, and also the several scrolls making up each division according to Hebrew reckoning or classification.

(1) *The Law.*—This is the earliest portion of the Hebrew Scriptures, and was regarded by them as the foundation stone in their religious life. The Hebrew term for law is *Torah*. This word is applied to the first five books of the Bible which the Hebrews believed were written by Moses. The Greek word *Pentateuch* is also applied to this section of the Hebrew Scriptures, the term meaning the five-fifths of the Law, or the five books. In the order of their arrangement they stand as follows:

Genesis, the Book of Beginning.

Exodus, the Book of Deliverance from Egypt.

Leviticus, the Book of Legal Requirements.

Numbers, the Book of Census Taking.

Deuteronomy, the Book of the Second Giving of the Law.

(2) *The Prophets.*—The section here mentioned was certainly the second step in bringing together "the oracles of God" by the ancient Hebrews. The word for prophet is *Nebi*, hence the Hebrew name for this group

of scrolls—the *Nebiim*. The writings regarded as belonging to this section, however, vary considerably from our English classification of the prophetical writings of the Old Testament. The Hebrews divided the group into two divisions, the first consisting of the *Former Prophets*, and the second, the *Latter Prophets*, as follows:

Joshua
Judges   } THE FORMER PROPHETS
Samuel
Kings

Isaiah
Jeremiah   } THE LATTER PROPHETS
Ezekiel
The Twelve

In this classification it should be explained that the scroll of Ruth was put with Joshua, Samuel included 1 and 2 Samuel, Kings included 1 and 2 Kings, and Jeremiah included the scroll of Lamentations. The twelve Latter Prophets are of course the Minor Prophets, as follows: Hosea, Joel, Amos, Obadiah, Jonah, Micah, Nahum, Habakkuk, Zephaniah, Haggai, Zechariah, and Malachi.

(3) *The Writings.*—Into this group were brought various sacred writings cherished by the Hebrews and faithfully preserved through the centuries. It is fairly certain that this section was the last to be set aside as a part of the Hebrew Scriptures. The Hebrew word *Kethubim*, meaning writings, is applied to these scrolls:

Psalms
Proverbs
Job
Song of Songs
Ruth
Lamentations   }   THE WRITINGS
Ecclesiastes
Esther
Daniel
Ezra and Nehemiah
Chronicles

In this list Chronicles includes of course our 1 and 2 Chronicles. Occasionally the scrolls of Ruth and Lamentations appear in this third section, but the Hebrews preferred them as listed under the Prophets. Attention is also called to the fact that five of the above scrolls were used for reading at the principal Jewish festivals both in the old days and in the time of Jesus.[5]

(4) *Arrangement of books in the English Bible.*—In the arrangement of books in the English Bible the Hebrew order disappears very largely, the emphasis being mainly on divisions according to subject matter. The English classification also features the individual books rather than combinations, the result being that where the Hebrews mentioned only twenty-two scrolls we have the thirty-nine which constitute our Old Testament— as follows:

Genesis
Exodus
Leviticus   } LAW
Numbers
Deuteronomy

---

[5]The five scrolls referred to are these: Song of Songs, used at the Passover; Ruth, the Feast of Pentecost; Ecclesiastes, the Feast of the Tabernacles; Lamentations, anniversary of the Fall of Jerusalem; Esther, the Feast of Purim.

Joshua
Judges
Ruth
1 Samuel
2 Samuel
1 Kings
2 Kings   } HISTORY
1 Chronicles
2 Chronicles
Ezra
Nehemiah
Esther

Job
Psalms
Proverbs   } POETRY
Ecclesiastes
Song of Solomon

MAJOR PROPHETS:
    Isaiah
    Jeremiah
    Lamentations
    Ezekiel
    Daniel

MINOR PROPHETS:
    Hosea
    Joel
    Amos   } PROPHECY
    Obadiah
    Jonah
    Micah
    Nahum
    Habakkuk
    Zephaniah
    Haggai
    Zechariah
    Malachi

3. *Preservation of Old Testament Writings*

In the early days of Israel the sacred writings were turned over to the priests, the sons of Levi, as their special care to be deposited in the tabernacle.[6] In all probability these writings consisted solely of the records written down by Moses. This statement is made in view of the fact that writing is not mentioned in Genesis in connection with any of the patriarchs (Abraham, Isaac, and Jacob); the first reference comes in the book of Exodus where Moses is commanded to record an incident in the course of the exodus from Egypt.[7] In later passages we are told repeatedly of the writings of Moses. In all of these references we are to understand that they described the sacred records of Israel, the oracles of God to his people through Moses. More pointedly than that, we may regard these early references as indicating the first division of the Hebrew Scriptures, the five books of Moses, substantially as we have them. It is entirely possible and probable that in the course of centuries these writings were edited as well as reverently guarded, but there is no proof to indicate that this was done on any extensive scale. The main point emphasized here is that, if any editorial work was ever done, it was done always under the eye of religious leaders and by competent scribes trained for that kind of work. Though we cannot trace every step of the long process, two outstanding facts reassure us of the great care taken in seeing that the sacred writings were preserved. First, there was the work of Ezra, the priest, the scribe, whose labors in connection with the Scriptures are described at length

---

[6]Deut. 31:9, 26.

[7]Ex. 17:14. While it is true that none of the patriarchs is said to have written anything, this should not be interpreted as meaning that they *could not* write. The art of writing was known among the ancient Egyptians and Babylonians at least 2,500 to 3,000 years before Abraham. Abraham himself was brought up in Ur of the Chaldees, a city whose culture was fully developed 1,500 years before he was born. The point here emphasized is that the Bible claims no writing for the patriarchs, but it does claim repeatedly that Moses wrote and that his writings were to be preserved. Compare Num. 33:2; Deut. 28:58; 31:9-13, 26; Joshua 1:7-8.

in Nehemiah.[8] In the second place, long before the time
of Ezra, during the days of Josiah, 621 B.C., we have a
like situation in which the writings and the scribes are
to the front.[9] We may believe that through all these
centuries, until the beginning of the Christian period,
the Hebrew Scriptures were in the hands of specially
trained men whose business it was to preserve them in
purity. The scribes of the New Testament, for example,
are pictured as being familiar with the Scriptures.

It is also certain that throughout these centuries the
text of the Scriptures became practically uniform. We
know now that a school of Hebrew scholars existed at
Tiberias in Palestine from about the first or second
Christian century, and that these scholars preserved the
Scriptures just as they found them. These scholars are
called the Massoretes. The text of the Hebrew Scriptures which they determined became the basis of the
Hebrew Old Testament. There is a Jewish tradition that
connects the Massoretes with the period immediately following the return of Ezra to Palestine. At any rate, by
comparing the Hebrew text with certain translations both
before and *after* the first century of the Christian era,[10]
we know that the text as we now have it is practically
the same as it was in the days of Jesus.

4. *Formation of Old Testament Canon*

The exact date for the formation of the Canon of the
Old Testament is not known. It is certain, however,
that long before the Hebrew people had any word to
express the Canon, the idea of a collection of sacred
writings was in existence. The term "canonization"
means the bringing together of these sacred books or
writings and regarding them as *authoritative* in matters

---

[8]Neh. 8:1-8.
[9]2 Kings 22:8-13.
[10]Reference is here made to the great translation of *The Seventy* in
Alexandria, begun about 285 B.C., and the Vulgate of Jerome, completed
about A.D. 405, both of which will be discussed later. To these might be
added the Samaritan Pentateuch, or the books of Moses, written in Old
Hebrew characters and originally dating at least to the time of Ezra,
458 B.C.

of religion. They were set aside as a standard of belief and practice and reverenced as the source of spiritual instruction. No other books stood in the same class, for no other writings were regarded as divinely inspired. In process of time the collection of Hebrew writings was completed and the Canon was regarded as closed, thus showing the special reverence given these books as the words of God to Israel.

On closer examination we find that the formation of the Old Testament was really a matter of growth, the beginning being placed in the early period of Hebrew history and the close after the return from the Babylonian captivity. In the early period is placed the Torah (that is, the Five Books of Moses, also called the Pentateuch). It is agreed by all that this section of the Hebrew Scriptures was not only the first, but the most important. In general, these writings are called the laws of Moses. Moses is regarded as the author of these books and there is no reason for denying that claim. That they were held in deepest reverence is shown by the finding of these laws in the Temple by Hilkiah the priest in 621 B.C., during the reign of King Josiah.[11] It should be remembered, however, that these writings had lain neglected through the centuries. It was their recovery that started a revival. Again, when Ezra and Nehemiah came with the Babylonian exiles to Jerusalem, they began to re-establish the religion of the Hebrews by calling the people back to the law of Moses.[12] When the Samaritan people were not allowed to have any part in the rebuilding program, they separated themselves permanently from the Hebrews and set up their own worship on Mt. Gerizim with the *Five Books of Moses as their Scriptures*. The date for this event is 458 B.C. At this time, accordingly, the Torah was clearly reverenced by both Hebrews and Samaritans.

The second division of the Hebrew Scriptures consists

---

[11] See 2 Kings 22:8 to 23:3.
[12] Neh. 8:1-8; 10:28-31.

of the Prophets whose written words were regarded with deepest reverence. The earliest of the writing prophets was probably Obadiah (about 845 B.C.), followed closely by Joel (830 B.C.), and Jonah (800 B.C.); while the latest was Malachi (430 B.C.), who appears in the period of the restoration with Haggai and Zechariah. During this period of about 415 years (i. e., 845 B.C.-430 B.C.) we must place all of the prophetical books of the Hebrew Scriptures with no later additions. The acceptance of all these books as sacred writings cannot be later than 400-350 B.C. as shown by the *Septuagint Version* of the Hebrew Scriptures which was begun in Alexandria in Egypt about 285 B.C. and which contained these various books. It is clear, of course, that this is the latest date possible, but the student must remember that hundreds of years intervened during which the writings of the earliest prophets (Obadiah, Amos, Hosea, Isaiah, Jeremiah, etc.) were cherished and consulted.

The third section of the Hebrew Scriptures, the *Writings,* falls in the latter part of Old Testament history, that is between the restoration and the dawn of the Christian era. Of course, many portions of these writings were produced in the early years (as early as the period of the Judges, David, Solomon, etc.) but were never placed on the same plane as the Law and the Prophets. But since these books appear likewise in the Septuagint (285 B.C.) they must be regarded as canonical before that date.

We may accept the outline given above as the probable manner in which the Hebrew Scriptures were brought together and finally canonized. As indicated, the process extends from the days of Moses (about 1425 B.C.) to the Septuagint, 285 B.C. In general, the Canon of the Old Testament was completed before 300 B.C.

II. THE NEW TESTAMENT

The collection of writings which we now call the New Testament originally consisted of separate letters or narratives written to churches, individuals, or groups of individuals other than churches, and which were circulated in the early Christian community. As a general rule, they bore the names of apostles or other outstanding members of the Christian circle, though in some cases no names are attached. Early tradition, however, identified most of these writers so that today we associate the various books with the men whose names they bear. At present it is fairly certain that all parts of the New Testament are correctly identified as to authorship except the epistle to the Hebrews which, though frequently attributed to Paul, is probably not the work of the great apostle. As all of these writings found their way into the several churches, they were cherished as inspired utterances of spiritual leaders, and came to be regarded as authoritative for the new faith both as to belief and practice. When they were brought together as the body of inspired writings for the Christian community they were at once put over in relation to the Scriptures of the Hebrews which they claimed to fulfil. The result was that the older writings became the *Old Testament* while the latter were called the *New Testament*.

1. *Language of the New Testament*

In view of the fact that Christianity was born in the midst of the great civilization of the Graeco-Roman world, we would expect to find that culture influencing the new religion in many ways. We are here concerned with only one aspect of that influence but, as will be seen, an extremely important aspect. Reference is made to the language of the New Testament, really the gift of Alexander the Great, who scattered the Greek language from one end of his vast kingdom to the other. Indeed, Greek was the world speech, understood in Rome, in Alexandria in Egypt, in Jerusalem, in Damascus, throughout Macedonia, Asia Minor, and all regions on to the Orient. Men could meet anywhere on the common basis of culture and speech. Greek was used in the courts, in the market places, in homes, in commerce, and in literature. Civilization was at a high point at the dawn of Christianity, and the new religion used the prevailing culture in its outward and onward sweep from Jerusalem to Rome.

Every book in the New Testament was written in the Greek. While other languages appear in several passages, these are so few as to be counted negligible. But the fact that Greek was employed indicates not only the widespread nature of that language, but also the general level of culture which must be considered as of high order. Whether the writings were sent to Rome, Philippi, Ephesus, the region of Galatia, Palestine, Syria, or elsewhere, Greek was the language of expression. Of equal significance is the fact that, with one exception, the men who wrote all these books of the New Testament were Jews whose mother tongue was Aramaic. The practical outcome was that the writers were using a foreign language, and their ability to do it so well reflects high culture. At any rate we must interpret properly that passage in Acts 4:13 which reflects the opinion of the Pharisees and Sadducees regarding Peter and John. They were neither unlearned nor ignorant, seeing that John became the author of five sections of the New Testament, and Peter of two, and that both authors wrote intelligently in a foreign language. Jude and James, the brothers of Jesus, wrote in Greek, and it is probable that our Lord himself spoke three languages. Matthew and Mark were full-blooded Jews, so was the author of Hebrews, whoever he was. Paul, the most highly educated of all the apostles, was a true son of Abraham, but he was perfectly at home in the language of the Greeks whether at Tarsus or at Athens. Finally, Luke is the only Gentile writer in the New Testament, probably a native Greek who lived at Antioch in Syria or at Philippi in Macedonia. All wrote in Greek, the language of the world in the first Christian century.

2. *Divisions of the New Testament*

Twenty-seven books go to make up the New Testament. These various writings were produced at different times and, as will be seen, written to meet special needs among the Christians of the first century. Regardless of the distinctions in time and purpose, however, there is a definite bond of unity which holds them together. In seeking to classify these writings there is some difficulty but, on the whole, the following groupings serve fairly well:

Matthew	
Mark	
Luke	THE GOSPELS
John	
Acts	} APOSTOLIC HISTORY
Romans	
1 Corinthians	
2 Corinthians	
Galatians	
Ephesians	
Philippians	
Colossians	
1 Thessalonians	
2 Thessalonians	
1 Timothy	EPISTLES
2 Timothy	PAULINE AND NON-PAULINE
Titus	
Philemon	
Hebrews	
James	
1 Peter	
2 Peter	
1 John	
2 John	
3 John	
Jude	
Revelation	APOCALYPSE

In this classification, the Gospels of Matthew, Mark, and Luke are called the Synoptic Gospels. The word "synoptic" means seeing together. The writers give their respective views of the person, life, and work of Jesus. John's Gospel is also historical in that it treats of the life of Jesus, but it is more of an interpretation of Jesus as the Son of God. Luke wrote Acts, a book which sets forth the record of Christian achievement through the Holy Spirit. All epistles, personal and general, Pauline and non-Pauline, are grouped together simply for convenience. Revelation, the final book, is of prophetic or apocalyptic order, and thus deals with the future or final triumph of the Christian movement.

3. Earliest Portions of the New Testament

In our study of the several parts of the Old Testament, attention was called to the time elapsing between the earliest books and the latest. The total period involved was seen to be about one thousand years, that is, from Moses (1425 B.C.) to the close of Old Testament prophecy (Malachi 430 B.C.). No very great expanse of time marks the earliest and latest portions of the New Testament. It will occasion surprise, perhaps, when the period in which *all portions* of the New Testament were produced is definitely stated as not more than *fifty years*. While it is true that every section of the New Testament was written during the first Christian century, it is equally true that all come between the middle of the century and its close.

It should be held in mind that the New Testament, as we now have it, is not chronologically arranged in the order of its books. Though there is no exact agreement regarding several points, the student will welcome at least a general summary for purposes of comparison and developments therein set forth. The following suggested dates will be found in general accord with conservative writers:[13]

---

[13]See Robertson's *Student's Chronological New Testament* for best arrangement of books and explanation.

James ....A.D. 52
Mark ....A.D. 52
1 Thessalonians .............................A.D. 57
2 Thessalonians .............................A.D. 57
1 Corinthians ...............................A.D. 57
2 Corinthians ...............................A.D. 58
Galatians ...................................A.D. 58
Romans ......................................A.D. 58
Matthew .....................................A.D. 62
Luke ....A.D. 62
Acts ....A.D. 50
Philippians .................................A.D. 50
Philemon ....................................A.D. 62
Colossians ..................................A.D. 62
Ephesians ...................................A.D. 62
1 Peter .....................................A.D. 65
2 Peter .....................................A.D. 67
Jude ....A.D. 67
Titus ....A.D. 67
1 Timothy ...................................A.D. 67
2 Timothy ...................................A.D. 68
Hebrews .....................................A.D. 69
John ....A.D. 85
1 John ......................................A.D. 85
2 John ......................................A.D. 85
3 John ......................................A.D. 85
Revelation ..................................A.D. 95

4. *General Purpose of New Testament Writings and Their Circulation*[14]

In the last conversation which Jesus had with the disciples, he charged them with the sacred mission of witnessing to the world regarding the facts of his life.[15] This they began to do in the city of Jerusalem, gradually pushing out to the uttermost part of the world. We understand that this witnessing in its early stages was, for

---

[14]For further study, see Carver's *How the New Testament Came to Be Written*. This book is now out of print. See your library.
[15]Acts 1:8-9.

the greater part, personal testimony. The disciples understood, however, that the span of their life would be short, and that the preservation of the facts of Jesus' life would have to take the form of written records. From the introduction to the Gospel of Luke, it is clear that there had been an unbroken account of apostolic tradition concerning these facts, and that many had already drawn up written records of some of the events that had taken place.[16] It is also plain that these accounts were made by those who were eyewitnesses and ministers of the Word. Of special importance among these eyewitnesses was the inner circle of the apostles themselves who were most vitally related to the events in the life of Jesus. They alone knew the facts. We may also conclude from Luke's statement that his purpose in writing to Theophilus was that he should be more accurately instructed regarding the things assuredly believed by all disciples. In general, this purpose underlies all of these writings in that they are designed to set forth the life of Christ and to give its explanation to the world in all respects.

There is no claim that we have in the New Testament all of the facts of Jesus. It is of interest, however, to state that it is our only source book of the life of Jesus. In all of these writings, including Gospels and epistles, there is the constant effort to explain the threefold mystery of *his Person, his suffering*, and *his kingdom*. His works and words are brought to the front always to illustrate and to confirm his wondrous claims. The power demonstrated in his miracles was clearly supernatural, and his words were divine. Indeed, it was the firm conviction of these disciples that the evidences growing out of the life of Jesus, his works, words, death, and resurrection fulfilled in every detail the Old Testament picture of the expected Messiah, the Saviour of the world. Add to all of this the experience of grace in their own lives, and the picture is complete.

[16]Luke 1:1-4.

With the rapid spread of Christianity from Jerusalem to the uttermost part of the world, there arose the necessity of preserving the story of Jesus for others, for those who never saw him in person or came in contact with the first circle of his followers in Palestine. In addition to this, there was pressing need that the new Christians should be instructed regarding the meaning of the facts of the life of Jesus, doctrinal beliefs, expectations, church affairs, daily conduct, and brotherly encouragement. As a consequence, the books of the New Testament gradually arose to meet all of these needs and were freely circulated among the early churches in close association with the cause of missions. In fact, it was the success of the missionary business that produced the New Testament; it was the answer of the Spirit to meet the growing needs of the kingdom of God. Regarded in this light, the New Testament easily lends itself to the following classification:

(1) *The Gospels.*—These are historical and biographical, giving some of the facts of the life of Jesus.

(2) *The Acts.*—Containing a historical sketch of the progress of Christianity in the first century.

(3) *Epistles.*—Setting forth the practical aspects of Christianity, as in the epistle of James, and certain epistles of Paul. They give useful suggestions regarding numerous problems arising in church administration; formal statements of Christian doctrine, as in Romans, Ephesians, Galatians, and John; defending the Christian religion against opposing groups, as in Colossians, 1 John, Hebrews, and other writings; encouragement in the face of serious persecutions, as in 1 Peter, Jude, Revelation, etc.

5. *Gradual Formation of the New Testament Canon*

Aside from the question of inspiration, it was not the feeling of the writers in the New Testament that they were producing books which would later be brought together to form what we now call the New Testament.

Except in Romans, Ephesians, and parts of Revelation, there is apparently no indication of the large importance which all of these writings were going to have in the development of Christianity. It is to be remembered, of course, that the Scriptures of the early Christians (including apostles and lay members of the churches), were the sacred writings of the Hebrew available to them both in the original Hebrew language and in the Greek version of the Septuagint. We know that they read the Septuagint and quoted it. To them it was the divinely inspired record of God's redemptive activity in relation to Israel and the Old Covenant. With the unique revelation of God in Christ, with the illumination of their understanding by the Holy Spirit, these men were led to see that what was foretold and foreshadowed in Hebrew Scriptures was now fulfilled in the life of Jesus, that the old dispensation had merged into the new, and that the Old Covenant was now giving place to the New Covenant. Accordingly, the body of writings which set forth the Hebrew expectations and experiences in redemptive history was now called the *Old Testament*, while the new writings concerning the new dispensation were called the *New Testament*. The rise of a New Testament necessarily involved the idea of an Old Testament. The distinction was made between the two sets of writings as early as the middle of the second century when Irenaeus, one of the church Fathers, employed the terms the Old and New Canons of Scriptures.

As in the case of the Old Testament Canon, the New Testament writings were gradually brought together into one collection. It was really a matter of growth. The earliest sections of the New Testament to circulate as a group were the Gospels, followed in turn by the epistles of Paul, and finally, the remaining parts. This development is clearly in view as early as Clement of Alexandria (A.D. 150) who distinguishes between the two groups of writings called *Gospel* and *apostle*, meaning, of course, the Four Gospels and the Pauline epistles. It

is of interest to note, also, that the earliest date given
for recognition of all the divisions of our present New
Testament goes back to Eusebius (A.D. 260-340). Gradually all portions of the New Testament were duly recognized as divinely inspired and authoritative, so that after
A.D. 397 no question was raised with regard to any division. All were accepted as the revealed and inspired
Word of God, whose unity of authorship is found in the
Holy Spirit, whose unity of subject is found in Jesus
Christ, and whose unity of fundamental beliefs and
practices is expressed everywhere. It was recognized
that this unity is not superficial but is rather inherent
in and essential to the records themselves. That conviction remains until today.

Finally, in the matter of canonization of the several
books of the New Testament to form the whole, we
must be careful to distinguish the process by which it
was done. Though many church councils or synods
made pronouncements regarding the books of the New
Testament, that is, as to what really constituted the
Canon of the New Testament, no church council or
synod ever had authority to make such a decree. The
church never determined the Canon of the New Testament; it had no right either to add to or to take from
that body of sacred writings which the enlightened conscience of Christians everywhere accepted as divinely
inspired. Any part that councils had was limited to
pronouncement as to what Christians everywhere were
already regarding as the Word of God. That is to say,
to canonize any book or books of the New Testament,
or to declare the whole book canonized, was not the business of the church or churches. The books of the New
Testament show their own inherent worth, and carry
their own marks of genuineness and trustworthiness.
These marks have been duly recognized through the centuries and are today as clearly embedded in these writings as when they were first produced in the first Christian century.

III. The Apocryphal Books

Before we close this chapter on the Canon of Scriptures, a word of explanation should be given regarding the Apocrypha, a body of writings held in high esteem by Hebrews two centuries before the Christian era and, later, by Christians themselves. Josephus, the Jewish historian, mentions these works in the following reference: "Our history hath been written . . . [i. e., the sacred history of the Jews as set forth in these various writings in detail from Artaxerxes to our own times], but hath not been esteemed of the like authority with the former . . . [forementioned books, i. e. the Canon of the Old Testament], because there hath not been an exact succession of prophets [i. e. inspired writers]."[17]

The meaning of the term "Apocrypha" is hidden or concealed, thus expressing the idea of *covered* or *veiled* references to coming events. They claim, of course, to be genuine writings and usually appear under the names of great characters in Hebrew history. The use of these names was intended to obtain a hearing for the messages set forth. But they never were accepted as inspired Scriptures by the Hebrews, though held in high esteem. It is certain that they were not incorporated in the original Septuagint at Alexandria, though later appearing in that version. Josephus never quotes the Apocrypha; Philo, a Jewish philosopher and religious teacher, does not use the Apocrypha, and no writer in the New Testament quotes directly from these works. Jerome (A.D. 385), when making the Latin Vulgate from the Hebrew and Greek Scriptures, at first refused to translate the Apocrypha as sacred scriptures, though he later complied with the request. It was through the Vulgate that the Apocrypha came into the English scriptures, being included even in the original King James Version of 1611. It is true that the Geneva Bible (English) of 1569 omitted the Apocrypha, it being the first to do so. Evan-

---

[17] Josephus, Against Apion, I. 8, p. 861.

gelical Christians reject the Apocrypha as authoritative utterances in matters of faith and practice, while usually holding them to be of high spiritual value for instruction. On the other hand, Catholic bodies accept these writings as on a par with other sections of the Old and New Testaments, and appeal to the Apocrypha in behalf of certain doctrines of the Church. It is known, of course, that the Bible of the Catholic Church retains these Apocryphal books while all modern English versions for evangelical Christianity omit them.

QUESTIONS FOR REVIEW

1. Explain the origin of the word "Bible."
2. What is the meaning of the term "Canon"?
3. To what people were the writings of the Old Testament given?
4. What is the language of the Old Testament?
5. Name the divisions of the Old Testament according to the Hebrew classification. What is the English Bible arrangement?
6. What were the earliest of the Hebrew sacred writings?
7. Did the Patriarchs leave any writings? Could they write?
8. Explain how the sacred writings of the Hebrews were preserved through the centuries.
9. Discuss the three stages in the formation of the Old Testament Canon.
10. What is the language of the New Testament?
11. Did the early disciples have any literary ability?
12. What are the divisions of the New Testament?
13. Name the earliest portions of the New Testament.
14. What was the general purpose of New Testament writings?
15. Discuss the formation of the New Testament Canon.
16. What is the Apocrypha? Is the Apocrypha included in our Bible? Give reason.

THE ANCIENT MANUSCRIPTS

OUTLINE

INTRODUCTORY

I. ORIGINAL WRITINGS OR AUTOGRAPHS

II. WORK OF SCRIBES AND COPYISTS

III. OLDEST MANUSCRIPTS OF THE HEBREW OLD TESTAMENT

IV. OLDEST MANUSCRIPTS OF THE GREEK NEW TESTAMENT

    1. The Vatican Codex

    2. The Sinai Codex

    3. The Alexandrian Codex

    4. Codex of Ephraem

    5. The Beza Codex

    6. The Washington Codex

    7. Other Capital Letter Manuscripts

V. LATER MANUSCRIPTS OF THE GREEK NEW TESTAMENT

THE ANCIENT MANUSCRIPTS[1]

INTRODUCTORY

In the three preceding chapters we have been chiefly concerned with the several steps in the growth and development of the Bible, beginning with revelation and inspiration and coming finally to the definite collection of the sacred Scriptures into the two Canons of the Old Testament and the New. The elementary facts in this process of Bible growth have been set forth, though no effort has been made to be exhaustive in their treatment. With proper understanding of these preliminary considerations, we are now in a position to take up other matters vitally connected with the backgrounds of our English Bible. As in other sections of this work we are not concerned with technical details, but rather seek to present the material in terms familiar to all. Fortunately, the modern generation of young students is much better equipped for such studies than the students of any preceding period, not only because of the thoroughness and scope of their instruction, but also because of the great wealth of biblical material made available during recent years. All of this helps us to understand the wonderful providence that has attended the giving and the preservation of the Bible through the centuries.

I. ORIGINAL WRITINGS OR AUTOGRAPHS[2]

No original writing by any author either in the Old Testament or the New is known to be in existence today.

---

[1]The term "manuscript" (abbreviated MS., plural MSS.) is derived from the two Latin words meaning "written by hand," as over against the printed works of later centuries. There are several kinds of manuscripts which will be presented in the following discussion.

[2]The term "autograph" is derived from two Greek words meaning the writing itself. It is of course applied to any narrative as it leaves the hands of the author. It is not a *copy* but the *original*.

In all probability all of these autographs have perished. Of course no one can say that none will ever be recovered, since many portions of ancient writings have been recovered from the sands of Egypt and from other sections of the Near East. But in view of the fact that the greatest care was taken in preserving copies of these original writings, the absence of autographs creates no very great difficulty. If the Magna Charta of the English people or the Declaration of Independence by the American Colonies were lost, so many genuine copies of their contents are in existence that no one would question their truthfulness or accuracy. It is also to be remembered that ancient peoples did not possess our modern conveniences of vaults and other types of safety boxes for precious papers. Even today we must exercise the greatest care in preserving state documents from the destructive forces of time and natural conditions. Hence, we do not marvel at the absence of autographs; in the process of time we would have expected all of them to disappear. On the other hand, we can be grateful that their value was so great that hundreds of copies were made, under the most trying conditions, and distributed in various parts of the world of that day. Indeed, so deeply were they reverenced by the faithful that no part of the inspired writings was ever allowed to be without many witnesses. We have literally thousands of copies in our hands today which prove the fidelity of the early Christians in handing down that which they had received. Whether the statement is applied to the New Testament or to the Old Testament, it is true that these writings are substantially the same as they were in the days of Jesus and the apostles.

II. Work of Scribes and Copyists

From the written records of ancient peoples we understand that the profession of the scribes was highly respected. Usually they were among the best educated people of their time. To them were committed important matters connected with the keeping of public records, and in the transaction of public business both at home and abroad. Royal decrees were drawn up by them and announced to the populace. Libraries and archives were placed under their control. No king went forth without his scribes who, in many cases not only recorded the chronicles of the sovereign's victories on temples and monuments, but actually inscribed them on the stone slabs of mountains here and there. In general, we may say that all historical records of the past head up in some way with the office of the scribe, and that it is due to him that we now possess our connected narratives of historical development in the ancient world.

In ancient Israel the scribe, while frequently concerned with state affairs, both military and secular, found his chief connection with the Word of God, the Scriptures. In this sense Baruch is the first scribe of whom we read, and Ezra the most outstanding.[3] To the scribes was committed the business of copying the law, of preserving the sacred writings in purity. We may hold confidently that they regarded this as a sacred duty and that they faithfully discharged their obligations. By the dawn of the first century the Massoretes come into view as the custodians and copyists of the Scriptures. As already noted it was the Massoretes who brought together the ancient Hebrew writings, determined the purity of the text, and produced the basic work which has underlain the Hebrew Old Testament since that period.

With reference to the New Testament writings, there was, of course, no school of Massoretes charged with the purification and preservation of the Greek Scriptures. The absence of any school of professional scribes, however, worked no serious disadvantages so far as preserving the purity of the New Testament was concerned. On the contrary it resulted in a marked advantage so that the numerous copies produced by the individual copyists may now be used to show with what accuracy they were

[3]2 Kings 25:19; Jer. 52:25; 36:4; Neh. 8:1.

made. The principle of safety in numbers is here illustrated. As will be shown later, the New Testament scribes did their work well, laboring under most trying circumstances and under real hardships. While it was almost impossible to avoid errors, whether intentional or unintentional, in text production, by comparing the various copies now in hand, we can detect the errors and consequently correct them. As a result we may have confidence that the New Testament books now in our hands are just the same as when originally produced by their authors.

III. Oldest Manuscripts of the Hebrew Old Testament

It was customary among the Jews to dispose of well-worn or disfigured scrolls of Scriptures. The first requirement, however, was that the scroll should be faithfully copied and proofed by many tests as to its correctness. Since the Scriptures were sacred, they had some feeling about destroying the writings by fire or other means, but were rather inclined to bury them with religious ceremonies. It is clear, of course, that as the old copies were disposed of, no ancient witnesses to the text probably ever will be found. If any old text has survived it would be more by chance than intention. And, so far as we know, no very old Hebrew manuscript is known to exist. The oldest portion of the Hebrew Scriptures in the world is now in Leningrad, Russia, and bears the date of A.D. 916. This particular manuscript is in the form of a book and includes only the prophecies of Isaiah, Jeremiah, Ezekiel, and the twelve Minor Prophets. Next in order is probably the manuscript of the Pentateuch in the British Museum (London) which is placed by some scholars as early as A.D. 856, but there is no agreement regarding this matter. Altogether we have about 1,700 manuscripts of the Hebrew Scriptures, including the complete Canon or its parts, though practically all are of very late dates. As already explained, the survival of only a few old manuscripts is the direct result of the Jewish custom of replacing the old works with the new. There is no likelihood that we shall find any earlier copies than those now in our possession. On the other hand, the text which has been handed down is practically the same as the Hebrew Scriptures in the first Christian century. It is even thought by some scholars that when the Massoretes at Tiberias determined the accepted text of the Old Hebrew manuscripts, they destroyed the older writings, leaving only the Massoretic text which is now standard.

IV. OLDEST MANUSCRIPTS OF THE GREEK NEW TESTAMENT

The case with manuscripts of the New Testament is entirely different. There was no special school of scholars to determine the accepted text of the New Testament or to fix the number of books to be included in the Canon. Immediately following the circulation of Gospels and epistles among the churches, scribes began to make copies for wider distribution and diligent study. As will be seen later, while the most important Greek manuscripts of the New Testament are placed about the middle of the fourth and fifth centuries, there are portions which are earlier. Among these appear the Old Latin Scriptures of the second century. We also know that there was an edition of the Four Gospels in Syriac about the second century. Of course all of these manuscripts were made from other manuscripts then in existence, thus giving rise to possibility of errors, intentional or unintentional, of omissions and additions. It is clear that copies of copies must have continued back to a reproduction of the original writings now lost. But the fact that we have these copies enables us to trace this process step by step to the threshold of the age of the apostles, to determine the main lines of text descent, to correct errors, to take out scribal additions to the earlier text, and thus to restore the writings of the New Testament to their original form and content. Though we have no autographs in our possession, the net result of research and criticism has been to present to students of the New Testament substantially the exact words of its several authors in the first century. This within itself is remarkable. It is also one of the outstanding evidences of our indebtedness to earnest scholars in their search for the truth.

While we cannot go into details regarding the oldest Greek manuscripts of the New Testament, the student is entitled to at least a summary of the leading facts. These writings are the most precious in the world. The fact that practically all of them are available in photographic copies, or facsimile, to scholars everywhere, is a mark of their value. We name the most important:

1. *The Vatican Codex*[4]

This manuscript is the chief treasure of the Vatican Library in Rome and is one of the three most precious biblical writings in existence. No one knows where it came from nor when it arrived in Rome. It is first referred to when Pope Nicholas V placed it in the Vatican Library between 1447 and 1455. From that time it was so closely guarded that no scholar was allowed to make extensive study of its contents. It was not until 1889-90 that photographic copies were made and their general use permitted. As a consequence, all scholars now have access to these reproductions which are found in leading libraries throughout the world. In the library of the Southern Baptist Theological Seminary, Louisville, Kentucky, there is a copy of this photographic reproduction, together with other facsimile manuscripts, and one genuine manuscript (parchment) of later date.

The Vatican Codex (indicated by the letter "B") consists of 795 pages, 10x10½ inches, and is written in

---

[4]The word "Codex" (plural, "Codices") comes from the Latin. Our word "code" is derived from the older term. Though applied here to the manuscripts, it really indicates a manuscript in *book form* as over against the *scrolls*.

66

6

Greek capital letters.[5] The material used for the manuscript is vellum which is a fine quality of leather made from calfskin or antelope, and very durable. The Codex contains practically all of the Old and New Testaments, the missing portions being in the book of Genesis 1:1 to 46: 28, Psalms 106 to 138, and all of our present New Testament after Hebrews 9:13. All scholars agree that this Codex is to be dated about A.D. 350 and that its age and accuracy make it probably the best in our possession.

2. *The Sinai Codex*[6]

In point of age and importance this manuscript stands next to the Vatican. It is dated about A.D. 375 though its discoverer placed it as early as A.D. 340. Written on the finest vellum, four columns to the page, in Greek capital letters, it consists of 346½ leaves. It is certain that it originally contained all of the Bible, though now lacking about one third of the books of the Old Testament. The New Testament is complete. It was discovered by Tischendorf in the Greek Catholic Monastery of St. Catherine (Mt. Sinai, in the Peninsula of Sinai) in 1844, but it took him about fifteen years to get possession of it. Through the influence of Czar Alexander II, of Russia, who was supreme head of the Greek Catholic Church, Tischendorf was permitted to take the manuscript to Europe. It was presented to the Czar of Russia, deposited in the Imperial Library in 1859. It remained in the possession of the Russian people until 1934 when it was purchased from the Soviet Government for the sum of $500,000, the amount being raised by the British Government and popular subscription. The Codex is now in the British Museum in London.

---

[5]The name for a capital letter manuscript is Uncial (pronounced un'-shi-al).

[6]The Codex Sinaiticus is frequently designated by *Aleph*, the first letter of the Hebrew Alphabet.

3. *The Alexandrian Codex*[7]

This is the third important Greek uncial manuscript of the Bible, its date being fixed at about A.D. 425. The Codex is supposed to have been made in Alexandria, Egypt, hence its name. It was given to King Charles I, of England, in 1627 by Cyril Lucar, patriarch of Constantinople. Its prior history is not known. The Codex consists of 776 pages, vellum, and contains the whole of the Old Testament and all of the New, except a few verses in Matthew, John, and 1 Corinthians.

4. *Codex of Ephraem*[8]

This manuscript has a fascinating history. Originally written in Greek capital letters about A.D. 475, and probably used for over six hundred years, it fell a victim to some zealous scribe who was so much impressed with the value of Ephraem's sermons that he erased the earlier writing from the vellum and wrote down the sermons instead. The term *Rescriptus* as applied to the manuscript suggests this scribal act, that is, "written over" or "written again." In view of the fact that vellum was very expensive, he probably did not hesitate in following this course. His act, however, suggests that the Codex did not stand as high in his esteem as in that of modern scholars. Fortunately, the ink used in the original writing was extra good, so that the attempt to erase only temporarily succeeded. By applying special chemical treatment to the manuscript, the faded letters came once again into view, thus enabling the scholars to read every word. The manuscript originally contained the whole Bible in Greek, but now only a few pages of the Old Testament survive together with about half of the New Testament. The manuscript is in the possession of the French people and is deposited in the National Library, Paris.

---

[7]Called Codex Alexandrinus and designated by the letter "A."
[8]The full name of this manuscript is the *Codex Ephraemi Rescriptus,* otherwise known as Codex *C.*

5. *The Beza Codex*[9]

The date given for this Codex lies between the fifth
and sixth centuries. It is written in capital letters (both
Greek and Latin) and consists of 415 pages of vellum.
For a long period the manuscript was not held in
high esteem, but during recent years has been rising in
favor. As just indicated, the Codex has two languages,
Greek and Latin, the left page being in Greek, the right
in Latin, one column to the page. It is the oldest known
manuscript with this arrangement. In content the Beza
Codex has only the Gospels and the Acts.

6. *The Washington Codex*[10]

While there are many highly prized biblical manuscripts in the United States, the Washington Codex has
the distinction of being the most important. It is written
in Greek capital letters on vellum and consists of 372
pages. In content the Codex includes all the Gospels
complete, arranged in the following order: Matthew,
John, Luke, and Mark. Nothing is known of its early
history. The date assigned to it is not later than the
fifth century, about A.D. 475.

7. *Other Capital Letter Manuscripts*

In addition to the six most important capital letter
manuscripts mentioned above, there are about 170 other
complete codices of the New Testament. To these might
be added more than one hundred other manuscripts of
the capital letter class representing only portions of the
New Testament. Of course all of these codices are in the
Greek language and date anywhere from A.D. 350 to
about the ninth century. These constitute naturally the
major or determining factors in fixing the text of the
New Testament.

---

[9]The Codex Beza, indicated by the letter "D." Obtained by Theodore
Beza from Lyons, France, and presented to Cambridge University Library
in 1581.
[10]Originally the Freer Manuscript of the Gospels, purchased by Mr. C. L.
Freer in Egypt in 1906, and now in the Freer Gallery in Washington, D. C.
It is designated by the letter "W."

V. Later Manuscripts of the Greek New Testament

In the former section our chief interest centered around the capital letter manuscripts of the New Testament and their extreme importance in determining the original text. But these uncial manuscripts are not all that we have in hand to do this work. From the ninth to the fifteenth centuries there appeared hundreds of Greek manuscripts in a "flowing" style, with letters joined together, to which we now apply the name "cursive." These are copies of the earlier uncial manuscripts and, accordingly, are not regarded as of equal importance in fixing the text, though a few are held in high esteem. The total number of cursive manuscripts recovered is now about 2,358 to which others are being occasionally added. Among these late additions is a genuine cursive in the possession of the Southern Baptist Theological Seminary, Louisville, Kentucky, consisting of the Four Gospels arranged as in our New Testament.[11] This is probably the second most important Greek manuscript of the Gospels in the United States at present, the Washington Codex being first. But all of them are of priceless value as surviving witnesses of the wonderful writings delivered to Christians in the first Christian century.

---

[11]Called the Robertson Codex, No. 2,358. Consists of 175 leaves (350 pages) of vellum. It is dated about A.D. 1000.

QUESTIONS FOR REVIEW

1. What is the meaning of the term "manuscript"? What is an *autograph*?

2. How many autographs of the Old Testament are in existence today? Of the New Testament?

3. Discuss the principal work of the Hebrew scribes.

4. Who were the Massoretes? What is their work called?

5. What are the oldest manuscripts of the Hebrew Old Testament? Where are they?

6. Why are there so few manuscripts of the Old Testament?

7. What is the difference between an uncial and a cursive manuscript?

8. What is a codex? Distinguish between a scroll and a codex.

9. Name the six principal manuscripts or codices of the New Testament. Where are they now? Describe each codex.

10. What is the Robertson Codex?

OLD VERSIONS

OUTLINE

OLD VERSIONS

INTRODUCTORY

The manuscripts which we have just reviewed take, of course, the highest rank in determining the accuracy and genuineness of the biblical text, both of the Old Testament and the New, and stand in the direct line of ancestry of our modern American Standard Version. Their chief value in the hands of present-day scholars, however, has been to clear up disputed points, to indicate the true meaning of words and phrases, to give more exactness in translation, and to correct intentional or unintentional errors of early copyists. The value of these manuscripts will increase with their age. But to our English forefathers, when they were struggling with problems of English Bible translation, not one of these great manuscripts was available. Indeed, all of the six aforementioned priceless codices were either unknown to or unused by revisers as late as the King James, or so-called Authorized Version, of 1611.[1] It should be quickly added that while this is a clear statement of fact regarding relations between revisers and the ancient manuscripts, it is altogether probable that the codices herein referred to had a more vital connection with the sources from which our Bible comes, i.e., the Versions. To these we now turn for brief study.

I. ORIGIN OF THE VERSIONS

The backgrounds of the Roman world into which Christianity was first introduced were powerfully influenced by the culture of the Greeks. Indeed, the world of that day was Graeco-Roman. The outstanding agent in this

---

[1]The *Codex Alexandria* was presented to King Charles I, in 1627, sixteen years after the King James Version was completed; the *Codex Ephraem* was not fully read until 1842; the *Codex Beza* was first published in 1793 and again in 1864; the *Vatican Codex* was made available to scholars in 1889-90; the *Sinai Codex* was recovered during the years 1844-52, and the *Washington Codex* of the Gospels was found in 1906.

cultural preparation for the coming of Christianity was
Alexander the Great, who not only conquered the countries of the Near and Middle East, touching even the
great river valleys of India, but also introduced throughout this vast territory the Greek way of thinking and
doing. One of the most important phases of his conquest
was the spread of the Greek language as the common
tongue among all the peoples included in his empire. It is
to Alexander that we owe the first effort ever made to
translate the religious literature of a people into a foreign
language, as in the reproduction of the Hebrew Scriptures
into the language of the Greeks at Alexandria in Egypt.
Incidentally, though this version (the Septuagint) was
designed primarily for the Jews in Alexandria, it later
became the possession of first century Christians who
used it freely both as individuals and in the churches.
It is also to Alexander the Great that we owe the language in which every book of the New Testament was
originally written. Later copies of these Greek writings
make up what we now call the great manuscripts of the
Greek New Testament. Of course it was from these
Greek manuscripts, probably some original writings from
the apostles, that some of the versions[2] were made.

Now, while Greek was the common language of ex-
change in various parts of the world during the first
century, there were two developments that made it necessary to employ other languages in spreading the story
both of the Old Testament and the New. *First*, with
the gradual growth of the power of Rome, its language,
the Latin, grew in favor and influence. Considerable
sections of the Empire, especially North Africa and
Western Europe, were more affected by the Latin than
by the Greek. The reproduction of the Scriptures in
these regions, therefore, would be mainly in the language
of Rome. Among these various Latin versions some are

---

[2] The term "version" is applied to any reproduction or translation of the
Scriptures into a language other than that of the original writing. All
English Bibles, being translations of Hebrew and Greek, are versions. The
same is true of all other translations. The term is distinguished from
"manuscript" which is an original or a copy of an original writing.

very early, particularly the Old Latin Version which appeared during the latter part of the second Christian century. And, *secondly,* with the rapid spread of Christianity there arose the urgent necessity of making the Scriptures available to other peoples in their own languages. As a consequence, numerous versions appeared in widely separated parts of the world. Some of these versions are of great value not only because of their early date, but also because they illustrate how faithfully the inspired writings were translated. *Finally,* it was in connection with this great movement of version production that our English forefathers came into possession of the Scriptures. And, as will appear later, it was from one of these versions that the first complete Bible was translated into our mother tongue. In the following summary, therefore, we consider it very important to set forth some of these early translations, and then to show in what way they were connected with the ancestry of our English Bible.

II. REVIEW OF PRIMARY VERSIONS

It is extremely important at this point that we keep clearly in view what is meant by primary versions of the Bible. As indicated in the Introduction to this book, there are now over one thousand languages and dialects into which the Scriptures have been translated either in whole or in part. The number increases every year. According to the meaning of the term, all of these are versions. The translation of any of these books into a language other than the original constitutes a version. But, while there are hundreds of versions in existence today, these are not considered primary, neither are the scores of translations circulated during the early centuries. Of this latter class, for example, one could select a most interesting and instructive list of versions, including the Coptic, Ethiopic, Armenian, Gothic, and Georgian all of which were made between the third and sixth centuries of the Christian era. To these might be added many others of great value. But practically all of these versions are based on earlier versions which we here designate primary. The following summary, while not exhaustive, will serve to introduce the most important of these works.

1. *The Septuagint*[3]

The translation of the Hebrew Scriptures into the Greek language during the reign of Philadelphus and his successors (about 285 B.C.-200 B.C.), was the most important religious event falling within the three centuries before the Christian era. It is said that Philadelphus, ruler of Egypt, was anxious to bring together all of the world's best writings and to place them in the great Alexandrian Library where more than 600,000 volumes or scrolls were collected and classified. It was his desire that no important piece of literature of any people should be overlooked. The Jews being invited sent their representatives who translated the entire collection of Hebrew Scriptures into the Greek. While there may be some basis for this account, it is more probable that the great Jewish population of Alexandria, having abandoned the Hebrew language for the Greek, since they were unable to read the Hebrew, demanded their Scriptures in a language that they understood. Whatever the explanation, the production of the Septuagint gave to the Jews, and later to the Gentile world, the first version of sacred writings of which we have any knowledge. The Septuagint was made from Hebrew writings already in existence and included all the books of Law, Prophecy, and Sacred Writings then accepted by the Jews as their Canon of Scripture. This collection of Scripture was accordingly already fixed and limited before 285 B.C. Of great importance to us at this point is the fact that when the Christians commenced to use the Septuagint to prove that Jesus was the Messiah foretold by the Hebrew prophets, the Jews gave up the Septuagint and proceeded to make other Greek versions to take its place. It con-

[3]Designated also by the Roman numerals LXX, meaning Seventy. The name was derived from the number of Jewish scholars who are said to have produced the translation in Alexandria, Egypt.

tinued to be cherished by the Christians, was widely distributed throughout the Roman world, and quoted freely by writers in the New Testament. It was on the basis of the Septuagint that the Ethiopic, Coptic, and other very early versions of the Old Testament were made.

2. *The Aramaic or Syriac Versions*

This was the language of Jesus and the disciples in Palestine. Originally spoken by people in Northern Syria and Mesopotamia, it displaced the Hebrew in Palestine after the restoration under Ezra and Nehemiah. It was closely related to the Hebrew. In all probability this explains why the early Hebrew Christians, though they had the Greek Scriptures in hand, desired to have them also in the Aramaic. With the spread of Christianity in Syria and Mesopotamia the native population would demand the writings both of the Old Testament and the New in their own language. The various steps in this movement are not clearly known at present, though it is agreed that the first Aramaic Version of the Old Testament was made about A.D. 150, or earlier; and that it was based on early Hebrew manuscripts. We also know that during the third century this Old Testament was widely circulated throughout Syria and that in content it was exactly the same as the Canon of Hebrew Scriptures.

In addition to the Syriac Version of the Old Testament, there was pressing need to present the Scriptures of the New Testament to the newly evangelized Syrians in their own language. There is a reliable tradition that, even in Palestine, Matthew wrote the sayings of Jesus in the Aramaic language though later his Gospel was certainly written in Greek. It is also of interest to mention here that the first *Harmony of the Gospels* was produced in the Syriac by Tatian about A.D. 160.[4] We have no copy of this work in its original form, though

---

[4]This work is called the *Diatessaron,* meaning by four. The Harmony consists of the ordinary arrangement of four columns showing the relation of Matthew, Mark, Luke, and John in subject matter.

two Arabic translations have survived as witnesses to its existence. It is also referred to in the commentary of Ephraem who died about A.D. 373. The production of this Harmony is the earliest publication of the Four Gospels that we know. It is clear, of course, that the Gospels were thus accepted as genuine at a very early date.

Finally, attention should be called to one other outstanding work in the Syriac that came to occupy the commanding position as the authorized text of the New Testament for Syrian Christians of the fourth century.[5] A few manuscripts of this version, dating from the fifth century, have survived. The original work is assigned to about the year A.D. 411.

3. Old Latin Versions

The history of the Old Latin Version of the Old Testament is not clearly known, though opinion of scholars now favors a very early date, about A.D. 150. It was not made direct from the Hebrew Scriptures but was based on the Septuagint Version already described. It was accordingly a translation of a translation but in spite of this disadvantage attained high merit. It is not known whether it was made in Syria or in North Africa. In all probability it came from Africa where Roman culture was very marked and powerful. There is no way of knowing exactly how widely the Old Latin was circulated though the evidences in hand point to North Africa, Syria, Italy, and other European countries. With the passing of time, many errors crept into the text (due to mistakes of copyists and scribes) so that a revision of the translation was demanded. This work of revision was assigned to Jerome who spent almost a quarter of a century on the task and whose work abides in our present Latin Vulgate.

4. The Latin Vulgate

The historic importance of the Latin Vulgate in the ancestry of the English Bible has hardly been recognized,

[5] Called the *Peshitta*, or "simple" version.

due probably to its present association with the Roman Catholic Church. But this great work by Jerome should be allowed to speak for itself and to be regarded in the light of its early mission, long before the Church had accepted it as its authorized Scriptures. For it is a fact well known that the Vulgate was rejected when first proffered to the early Christians by Jerome, after the most devoted and sacrificial labors, and that the author himself died of a broken heart. But the Vulgate went on, gradually winning its way by merit over the inferior translations of the day until accepted by the Church as the authorized Latin Bible of all Roman Catholic bodies.[6] But it is not with these facts that we are chiefly concerned, for, apart from its prime position in the Church of Rome, the Vulgate is seldom mentioned among evangelical bodies today, nor are English-speaking Catholics acquainted with it except through English translations. We are concerned, however, in pointing out to the present generation of Bible students that our English or Anglo-Saxon forefathers, as well as other groups of early peoples in Western Europe, first received the enlightenment of the Scriptures largely through the pages of the Latin Vulgate.[7] It was, of course, not the only source of biblical instruction, but it was the most important through the early part of the Middle Ages of Europe (about A.D. 500-1500). Of special importance in this connection is the fact that the first complete Bible in English was a translation of the Latin Vulgate by John Wycliffe A.D. 1383. Prior to Wycliffe's day it was the sourcebook from which other Fathers were translating portions of Scripture into English. Today, of course, we are in no sense dependent on the Vulgate, nor does it enter into the determination of our English text, but its early mission should not be overlooked. Jerome

---

[6]Adopted by the Council of Trent, April 8, 1546.
[7]The word means to make general or accessible to all. The Vulgate, including the Old Testament and the New, was made by Jerome from the Hebrew and Greek manuscripts mainly, though he used somewhat the Septuagint and also the Old Latin already in existence. Of course he was a scholar of the first rank. The Vulgate was begun in A.D. 383, and completed in A.D. 404. Jerome labored mainly in Bethlehem, Palestine.

was one of the great men in Bible translation, a scholar of the first rank, who did his work in a masterful way though he never lived to see it fully accepted by his generation. In later centuries, on the other hand, its influence would extend to regions and peoples of whom he had no knowledge.

QUESTIONS FOR REVIEW

1. Distinguish between a manuscript and a version.
2. What aspect of Alexander the Great's work contributed to the spread of the Scriptures?
3. What developments made it necessary to translate the Scriptures in other languages?
4. What is a primary version?
5. Describe the origin of the Septuagint Version of the Hebrew Scriptures.
6. Was the Septuagint used by early Christians?
7. What was the first *Harmony of the Gospels?*
8. What great work came from the hands of Jerome? When? Where?
9. What were the sources from which the Latin Vulgate was made?
10. When was the Vulgate accepted as the authorized Bible by the Roman Catholic Church?
11. What was the position of the Vulgate in the religious life of our forefathers?

EARLY ENGLISH PARAPHRASES AND TRANSLATIONS

OUTLINE

EARLY ENGLISH PARAPHRASES AND TRANSLATIONS

INTRODUCTORY

As we begin to examine more carefully the various steps in the development of our modern English Bible, it is well to refresh ourselves with the glowing tribute uttered by Sir Walter Scott when requesting his attendant to bring him the Book. In view of the fact that the library of the great writer consisted of hundreds of volumes, the attendant embarrassingly answered, "which book is meant, Sire?" "There is but one Book," replied Sir Walter, "the Bible." By every standard of merit and of greatness that estimate has been fully justified. Printed in more languages, read by more people, and earnestly consulted in more ways for heavenly counsel than all other books combined, the Bible is, and certainly will remain, the greatest book in the world. To all it carries the story of God's love for the human race, the account of his unceasing activity for the welfare of men, and the offer of merciful provisions both as to salvation from sin and restoration to a life of useful service in his kingdom. It is a living Book, charged with the message of life, and inspired throughout by the indwelling Spirit who directed men in producing and preserving its records. As we have seen, this message finds its historical connection with Israel in the call of Abraham and the spiritual development that followed him, until the birth of Jesus in Bethlehem of Judea. The wonderful unfolding of this redemptive movement is clearly outlined for us in the pages of the Old Testament where we have its beginnings, its delays, and the gradual realization of the ends in view; while in the books of the New Testament we have the glorious fulfilment in the events of the life of Jesus and in the continued labor of his followers

in the cause of missions during the first Christian century.

Now it is one of the wonders of his love that such a
story should ever have been written, and one of the
miracles of his grace that it should ever have reached *us*.
Indeed, while we easily speak of the English Bible as our
heritage, it is more than that; it is an *achievement*,
marked by sacrifices far removed from the knowledge
and experience of the modern generation. The Bible was
not handed down to us any more than it was handed
down to Hebrews or early Christians. Every step in its
survival was taken through a maze of misunderstanding
and jealousy, suspicion and misrepresentation, harsh
words and actual combat, imprisonment and banishment,
fire and sword, life and death. That it has survived is
due solely to the grace of God in sustaining loyal hearts
in a devout and divine cause. The history of that struggle is the history of our Bible. Its fascination, romance,
and inspiration can never lose their appeal nor fail to
kindle gratitude in the heart of every student of the
Word.

1. The Bible Among the Anglo-Saxons

The introduction of the Scriptures among the early
Britons and Saxons is a matter still shrouded in a great
deal of mystery. The evangelization of the Britons might
have occurred as early as the second century in connection with the Roman army of occupation in which there
were probably some Christians.[1] We are on firmer
ground at the beginning of the fourth century when it
is definitely known that Christianity is exerting strong
influence in Britain. In these early centuries, up until
the sixth, the Britons were free from the power of any
church control, being left entirely to themselves to work
out their own problems. They were strongly missionary
as evidenced in the progress of the gospel in Britain,

[1]The invasion of Britain by the Romans under Julius Caesar took place
in 54 B.C. It was unsuccessful. During the reign of Claudius, the fourth
Roman Emperor, Britain was occupied by the Romans, A.D. 44.

Ireland, and Scotland, and in a later movement when Irish-Scotch missionaries penetrated Germany, Switzerland, and the Italian Alps with the message. At the time of the Saxon invasion of Britain (about A.D. 450) the native population was pushed into the more secluded regions of the west and northwest where they gave themselves to the development of their own religious life. It is fairly certain that the Britons made no effort to evangelize the Saxon invaders who had driven them from their homes. In later years, during the papacy of Pope Gregory the Great (590-604), a missionary crusade was undertaken by Augustine who claimed the conversion of the king of the Saxons with 10,000 of his subjects and brought them into subjection to the Roman Church. Later, being zealous to convert the Britons, the missionaries directed a military campaign in which about three thousand British Christians were slain by the Saxons. Though they were never conquered by these strong-arm measures, there was a gradual merging of the Britons with the Saxons and other newcomers to make the distinct type of Anglo-Saxon. It is in this period that we can trace more accurately the matters connected with Bible paraphrasing and translation.

One other point should be presented. As already stated, we do not know the earliest versions of Scriptures to reach the peoples of Britain. In any case the general condition of illiteracy would create no demand on the part of the people for the written word. On the other hand, there was always need for an instructed clergy and this need was partly met by the clergy themselves. With the coming of Roman influence, though the language barriers of Angles, Jutes, and Saxons were being removed, Latin remained the official and religious language of the region. At this time the Latin Vulgate was introduced as the first Bible of our forefathers, and remained the principal source of religious instruction until the days of Wycliffe. There was no disposition on the part of the Church to encourage laymen in examining the Scriptures, even if they had been able to read the

Latin, nor to provide the people with a translation in their own tongue. Unfortunately, that has never been the policy of the Roman Church, for, even when permission to read is given, the lay member has no right to private interpretation. On the contrary, the policy of all evangelical bodies has been to encourage Bible reading and study and to make the Word of God available to everyone in his own language. Our English forefathers recognized the wisdom of Bible translation so that all might have direct access to the Word of God apart from priest, church, or other medium. That has remained the conviction of our people through the centuries.

II. CAEDMON, THE FORERUNNER[2]

No one should despise the day of small beginnings. Long before the Pyramid of Cheops, the great wonder of the world, lifted its head to the skies, early Egyptians learned the principles of its construction when making their lowly graves. It is a long journey from the cave-dwellers and cliff-dwellers to the Empire State Building, but the way is plainly marked step by step. In the growth of English Bible translation the story is no less remarkable. Its beginnings could hardly be pictured in lowlier circumstances. As the Lord of life began his earthly career from the manger, so the earliest form of biblical literature in our mother tongue was lifted from the stable. The story, centering around Caedmon, a Saxon shepherd, is well known and never fails to attract both young and old. Embarrassed by the gifts of his fellows in banquet halls who readily sang their songs to the accompaniment of the harp, Caedmon always retired before his turn came. After one of these experiences he had a vision of the risen Lord who said to him, "Sing me a song." "I cannot sing," replied the shepherd, "for this cause it is that I came hither." "Yet shalt thou sing to me," said the Lord. "What shall I sing?" The vision replied, "The beginning of created things."

---

[2]Caedmon lived about the latter part of the seventh century or A.D. 670.

From that time Caedmon began his work of paraphrasing.[3] Being unable to read the Latin Vulgate, he
was dependent on others to translate for him the Bible
story into his native language. This service was done by
the Abbess of Whitby as a rule, though the monks in the
Abbey also assisted. It is said that when Caedmon
heard these stories he immediately composed beautiful
paraphrases to the musical accompaniment. He sang of
the creation of the world, man, history of Israel, the life
of Jesus, and the joys of the kingdom of heaven. The
common people heard him gladly. It is to Bede that we
are indebted for facts concerning the life and work of
Caedmon. These accounts are given in his *Ecclesiastical
History of England.*[4]

The student will be interested in the following example of Caedmon's paraphrases, based on the appearance
of Jesus to the disciples by the Sea of Galilee:

> For he went forth
> the Lord of Angels,
> in the strong city,
> and bade fetch
> angels all bright
> and even bade say
> to Simon Peter
> that he might on Galilee
> behold God
> eternal and firm,
> as ere he did—
> Then as I understand, went
> the disciples together
> all to Galilee,
> inspired by the Spirit,
> The holy Son of God,
> whom they saw
> were the Lord's Son.[5]

[3]The word means making a restatement of a passage, a free rendering.
or fuller explanation.
[4]Chapter XXIV. See your library.
[5]Thorpe, *Caedmon's Paraphrases.* This book is now out of print. See
your library.

As already indicated, Caedmon's work is not to be considered as a translation, though it was certainly the first step in putting the Scriptures into our mother tongue. His paraphrases have no critical value, but express the ambition of a great heart to give the Word of God to his own people. More illustrious men, possessed of high education and culture, will follow in his steps, but each must trace the progress of Scripture translation to this extraordinary "son of the soil."

III. The Venerable Bede

Caedmon, the father of Anglo-Saxon poetry and forerunner of English Bible translation, died in 680. Bede was then about seven years of age (A.D. 673-735). He thus followed closely in time the man whose story he was going to tell in his history of England, and whose beginnings in biblical literature he was going to crown with great glory. Bede, when a child seven years of age, was adopted into the Abbey of Wearmouth and later taken to Jarrow where he lived the remainder of his life. In this classical and religious environment he followed his profession as a consecrated monk. He was the most famous scholar of his day, versed in the literature of Greece and Rome, and familiar with the science of medicine, astronomy, rhetoric, and other branches of knowledge. In the modern age we delight to refer to him as the father of English Ecclesiastical history, while also knowing that we are indebted to him for our earliest accounts of English economic and political history. Indeed, the work of Bede, plus the Anglo-Saxon chronicles which continued his history, provides England with reliable sources of its beginnings such as no other European nation possesses.

But the great learning of Bede was not given solely to the advancement of the sciences, for in his profession of teaching he was more interested in religion, in the study of the Scriptures, in translation and interpretation. Prepared as no other man of his period, it was in the field of religion that he made his greatest contribution. At the close of his church history he thoughtfully added a summary of his literary work, the list including sermons, commentaries, and translations relating to more than twenty-five books of the Old Testament and practically all of the New Testament. We know that on the last day of his life he completed a translation of the Gospel of John. No part of this translation has been preserved.

All of the works referred to in the preceding summary make up only about half of Bede's writings. He was a man of exceptional ability and insight. His literary productions not only had wide range but great merit. His popularity was marked in his own monastery where he was greatly beloved for his humility and deep learning, and extended to the larger field of the English world of letters.

IV. The Ambition of a Good King

In the modern age there are usually so many sources from which to gather facts of the lives of great men that the student of history has little trouble in selecting material for special purposes. In the early days, however, historians were few and the accounts which they have left are not always full or complete. This is true regarding the life of Alfred the Great (849-901), one of the outstanding men among the early Anglo-Saxon rulers. Various traditions have been handed down concerning his many good qualities and deeds. It is specially mentioned that he was deeply religious, and that he was much concerned about giving the Scriptures to his Anglo-Saxon people in their own language. It is highly probable that he did some of this translation work himself. At any rate we can believe that he was responsible for it. Regarding this work special reference is made to Alfred's Dooms which consisted of the Ten Commandments translated into Anglo-Saxon, and which were made fundamental in Anglo-Saxon life. In addition to the Commandments, the Lord's Prayer was beautifully rendered into the common language, also some of the Psalms. It is perhaps true that King Alfred did not enter the field of Bible translation as a scholar, on the order of Bede, but he was so deeply interested in the Bible for his people that he made every effort to bring it within their reach. In this respect he is outstanding in the history of English Bible development and is placed after Bede in the order of his achievements.

V. Archbishop Aelfric

The earliest known version of the Gospels in our mother tongue is the *interlinear Anglo-Saxon* of the *Lindisfarne Gospels* whose date is about A.D. 950; originally made from a Latin text brought from Europe about 670 and based on the Vulgate of Jerome. The interlined language, the Anglo-Saxon, was of course designed for the benefit of English-speaking people who were not acquainted with the Latin. On the other hand, the earliest known copies of Anglo-Saxon Gospels, without Latin texts, date from about the tenth century. The oldest and most valuable of these was made by Aelfric (then an abbot, but later Archbishop of Canterbury) about A.D. 1000. In addition to this work, the Archbishop is also credited with Anglo-Saxon translations of the Pentateuch, Joshua, Judges, Esther, Job, and a portion of Kings. The exact sources of his translations are not known though he might have had several at hand. Aelfric stood right on the threshold of the Norman period of invasion and conquest of England. Practically all of his works have perished though we are fully informed of their extent and importance in Bible translation. Aelfric died about A.D. 1006.

VI. Period of the Norman Conquest

The invasion of England by William of Normandy in 1066 was one of the most far-reaching events in English history. While the results of this conquest may be traced in numerous ways, particularly in the social, economic, and political conditions, we are chiefly concerned now with its general bearing on the movement of English Bible translation, and, also its influence on the English language itself. On close examination these two results will be found very significant.

In the first place, we have seen that the translation movement on the whole had been very slow. The period of time between the two great figures of Caedmon and William of Normandy is 332 years, but at no point during the three centuries can it be said that the Bible had had free circulation among the Anglo-Saxon people. The work of Caedmon, Bede, Alfred, and Aelfric was of vast importance and marked great advances in the direction of giving the people the Scriptures in their own tongue. There were many obstacles in the way. The people themselves were limited from an educational standpoint; there were only a few well-equipped scholars to do the work, and the period altogether was one of frequent changes. Angles, Jutes, Danes, and Saxons, with many other elements, were contending for the field so that language itself was not fixed. Numerous dialects in various sections of the country offered little encouragement for versions of the Scriptures. When William of Normandy ruled, confusion was everywhere. Naturally when William conquered England he decreed many reforms or changes which he tried to put into effect even by force of arms. Among these changes was the outlawing of Anglo-Saxon as the native language and the substituting of the Norman-French, the language of the conquerors. All outward movements toward native versions of Scriptures were therefore put under royal ban. As a consequence the years immediately following these measures hardly witnessed any marked progress in translation. This was clearly providential, for any work done with such differences in language conditions would not have been of long duration. Three more centuries will pass before order will come out of this confusion.

In the second place, William's bold attempt to outlaw the language of the native Anglo-Saxon peoples was doomed to fail. The Norman invaders, few in number as compared with the native population, could not always retain their distinct racial marks but would become lost in the Anglo-Saxon strain. That outcome was expected. In like manner the complete removal of the native language from native soil was impossible, though changes would certainly be made both as regards the imported language and the native. As a consequence the two languages ran along independently for a season but gradually were found leaning toward each other; differences were being toned down, and adjustments made. Indeed, so many other similar processes of leveling were going on that at the end of two and a half centuries the English language stood out rather clearly and distinctly. At the end of this period a master workman, John Wycliffe, stands waiting to use the English language in the making of the first complete English Bible ever written.

QUESTIONS FOR REVIEW

1. In what sense is the English Bible our heritage? In what sense an achievement?

2. Tell something of the early experiences in the religious life of the Angles and Saxons.

3. Describe the work of Caedmon. What is a paraphrase of the Scriptures?

4. What contribution did Bede make to the spread of the Scriptures among the Anglo-Saxon people?

5. Who was Alfred the Great?

6. What is the earliest known version of the Gospels in our mother tongue?

7. Was the English language fixed during the period from Caedmon to William of Normandy?

8. What was the result of the Norman Conquest on English Bible translation?

ENGLISH VERSIONS

OUTLINE

INTRODUCTORY—FACTORS AFFECTING BIBLE TRANSLATION

1. The Attitude of the Church
2. The Needs and Demands of the People
3. Devotion of Scholars
4. Royal Opposition Overcome
5. Invention of the Printing Press
6. The Revival of Learning
7. Religious Reformations
8. Growing Unity
9. Discovery of New Material
10. The Changes in Language

I. WYCLIFFE'S VERSION (1382)

II. TYNDALE'S VERSION (1525)

III. COVERDALE'S VERSION (1535)

IV. THE GREAT BIBLE (1539)

V. THE GENEVA BIBLE (1560)

VI. THE BISHOPS' BIBLE (1569)

VII. THE ROMAN BIBLE (1582-1609)

VIII. THE KING JAMES VERSION (1611)

IX. THE REVISED VERSION (1885)

X. THE AMERICAN STANDARD VERSION (1901)

XI. THE REVISED STANDARD VERSION (1946 AND 1952)

XII. MODERN TRANSLATIONS

ENGLISH VERSIONS

INTRODUCTORY

The early period of English Bible history which we have just reviewed, that is, the period extending from Caedmon to the Norman Conquest, may be properly termed an era of unrest and preparation. During this period of almost four hundred years there was hardly any settled government among the peoples of the British Isles; the several tribes were very hostile to one another; foreign invasions were frequent, and general conditions uncertain. In the matter of a common language, the situation was not greatly improved. Now and then some scholars of high rank would appear, but, with the several dialects of the people struggling for survival, no unified language was yet possible. It is true that the outlook for a common language was fairly bright about the ninth and tenth centuries, but the Norman-French invasion brought all progress in that direction to a sudden stop. The purpose of William the Conqueror was to introduce on a wide scale Norman-French customs and, if possible, to compel the native people to abandon the Anglo-Saxon language in favor of the Norman-French. There followed, of course, another long period of unsettled conditions when the two languages struggled for survival side by side. Fortunately, however, time is a great factor in breaking down barriers and in bringing together elements of wide differences. Thus it happened that the two groups of peoples, the Norman-French and the Anglo-Saxon, were slowly drawn together and were actually united both in blood and culture. The language that was born of this union was the English, our mother tongue. But its development was gradual and natural, and stretched through a period of about three hundred years.

Now the later period of English Bible history, that is, from the Norman Conquest to the modern age, witnessed many changes, some favorable and others unfavorable to Bible translation. Since these are factors that have greatly influenced the whole course of English Bible history, a word of explanation should be given regarding the most important.

1. *The Attitude of the Church*

The Roman Catholic Church was firmly established in England during these centuries. In common with religious conditions in Europe proper, Christianity suffered great abuses in England during the thirteenth, fourteenth, and fifteenth centuries. Corruption was found in all places, and even the clergy did not measure up to its high spiritual mission. In the midst of such unfavorable conditions the Church was not at all concerned with the spread of the Scriptures in an effort to improve the spiritual life of the people, but, on the contrary, actually discouraged and forbade the circulation of the Bible among the laymen. It should be understood, however, that while this summary applies specially to the Catholic power in England, the same attitude was continued by the Church of England through a considerable period. Of course the Church of England abandoned this policy in later years and became the leading factor in Bible translation for the English people.

2. *The Needs and Demands of the People*

It was to a very great extent the needs and demands of the common people that changed the attitude of the Church on the question of Bible translation. With the growth of education among the people there was a demand for the Scriptures in their own language. The Bible was available to the clergy since they were the authorized interpreters of the Word of God, but the people did not have the Book in their hands. Church ser-

vices were all conducted in the Latin, the great majority
of worshipers not knowing what was being said. It was
not the purpose of the Church to shed light for the ignorant but really to encourage dependence on the Church in
every phase of life. Great cathedrals and wonderfully
decorated interiors, the confessional, elaborate ritual,
feasts and festivals, penance, pilgrimages, superstitious
practices, and above all, the unchanging sacraments—all
these bound the people to church authority and discouraged individuality and independence. The whole system
was so bad that Wycliffe could say that the great need
was that all believers should know "what are the true
matters of their faith by having the scriptures in a
language which all may understand."

3. *Devotion of Scholars*

Not many men in these early centuries were capable
of doing the work required in Bible translation. There
was a great deal of ignorance even among the clergymen. Of course, there were exceptions both among the
schoolmen and the clergymen. In the Anglo-Saxon period we have seen the outstanding work of Bede and
King Alfred, followed by that of Bishop Aelfric. Three
centuries after the Norman Conquest, Chaucer, the father
of English poetry, was flourishing, but he was not concerned with Bible translation. In this same period John
Wycliffe, "the scholar of Oxford," appeared, leaving
behind him the splendid achievements of his lifework in
the field of Scripture translation. Later still William
Tyndale, sixteenth century, the greatest scholar of his
era, laid down his life in the cause of Bible translation.
To these men and others we are under lasting obligation.

4. *Royal Opposition Overcome*

Unlike Alfred the Great, many of the kings set themselves on the side of the Church and against giving the
Scriptures to the people in their own language. Royal
decrees always were backed, of course, by the power

of the state to enforce. In 1388 the king decreed that "no person should keep, transcribe, buy or sell books, treaties or pamphlets by John Wycliffe." In 1395 an effort was made by Parliament to annul the Bible, and in 1401 English Bibles were ordered to be burned. Indeed, during these days people had to secure licenses to possess a Bible. But all of this opposition was overcome in time so that by 1611 King James issued the Authorized Version which became the outstanding Bible of English speaking people.

5. *Invention of the Printing Press*

The invention of the printing press about 1450 had a profound bearing on the Bible. Prior to this great event all Bibles had been written by hand at great cost both in time and money. Actually only well-to-do people could afford to own the Scriptures. Poor people purchased the right to read or to have read to them portions of Scriptures for definite periods of time. The great masses, however, had no contact with the Scriptures in English. The printing press changed all of this. The first book to issue from the printing press was a Latin Bible. The first complete Bible printed in English was Coverdale's in 1535. Since 1450 about one billion Bibles, or portions of the Bible, have been printed in over one thousand languages and dialects.

6. *The Revival of Learning*

This great movement which witnessed a rebirth of the ancient culture of Greece and Rome, particularly in architecture, sculpture, and literature, and which spread from Italy through other parts of continental Europe and to England, was attended by a revival in religion and in the Bible. An age which saw the discovery of the New World also saw the rediscovery of the spiritual life and the value of the individual to God. The new learning of the Greeks and Romans, when it came out of the forgotten past, handed to the world a new Bible and a new spirit. Its contributions were greatest probably in the reformations experienced in England and in Germany.

7. *Religious Reformations*

The Church was gradually losing its hold on thoughtful people and these in turn were influencing the great masses. Religious decline could be seen in all countries. Spirituality was cheapened by abuses growing out of penance and confessional, and by external conformity with a dead ritualism. The individual was pressed down, forbidden to think for himself in matters concerning his soul, and urged to depend on others to do his thinking for him. The Bible was never intended for the masses but only for the Church to interpret through its priests to the masses. Unrest was seen everywhere. With Martin Luther the Great Reformation began in Germany, but in other European countries religious revival was no less strong and effective. The circulation of the Bible not only encouraged reform but actually produced it.

8. *Growing Unity*

Men of the various countries were beginning to see that they had much in common. The ends of the world were gradually meeting in the new discoveries and the sympathies of the people were being broadened. Social, religious, commercial, and political conditions were undergoing change and in all of this movement the achievements of one part of the world came to be shared by another. The spirit of common interests was abroad, and brotherhood was beginning to bear fruit. In all of this movement, both in producing and supporting it, the Bible was at the foundation.

9. *Discovery of New Material*

There is always keenest interest in the discovery of any material bearing on the Bible and the Bible story. Of special interest is the finding of old manuscripts such as we have described in chapter 4 of this work. In our modern times this phase of Bible study has steadily increased in interest for all students. All of the great manuscripts have come into our hands since the days of the King James Version. In addition we have thousands of other literary sources both for the Old and New Testaments which our forefathers never thought were in existence. All of these discoveries lead on to a continual process to give to the Scriptures their original form and meaning.

10. *The Changes in Language*

Finally, our own language is constantly undergoing changes. Words that were perfectly understood as late as the King James Version in 1611 are now practically foreign. We no longer use them to express the ideas which they formerly carried. In addition to changes in meaning and in the passing of words into non-use, new words are being added each year. It is these occurring changes that make it necessary at various periods to issue new versions of the Bible. In the past few years several attempts have been made with this end in view, the results of which are stated in a later section of our studies. It is clear that changes will always take place and that the future will witness other versions.

The foregoing summary gives a fair idea of the many factors in the background of the several versions of the English Bible to which we now turn. Not all of these developments took place at the same time but are seen extending through the centuries. In the earlier period there was no real danger confronting the translator who sought to make the Scriptures available in the Anglo-Saxon, but beginning with Wycliffe there was bitter opposition and even persecution. As the story unfolds, however, we will witness the loyalty of honored and devout men who stood by their tasks and who, in the long run, prevailed, though some of them never lived to taste the fruit of their victories. In reviewing these men

and their work we must necessarily be brief, but it is
hoped that the main steps during the centuries from
Wycliffe to the present will be made plain to all.

I. WYCLIFFE'S VERSION (1382)

John Wycliffe was called by his enemies "John Wicked-
Believe," and branded as a heretic and traitor to the
Church which he served as parish priest at Lutterworth.
He is held today in grateful memory as the *father of
English prose, the morning star of the reformation, and
the flower of Oxford scholarship*. To him we are indebted for the first complete Bible in the English language. He was a fearless reformer, courageous in
protesting abuses against the common people whether
committed by the Church, the crown, or the clergy.
Wycliffe was a man of high ideals and stern character,
against whom no enemy could ever bring a damaging
charge. It was the great ideal and passion of his life to
give the people the Bible in their own language as over
against the Latin which many heard but few ever understood. His great conviction, "I believe in the end the
truth will conquer," was the secret of all those splendid
things growing out of his sufferings and his successes.
Single-handed he won in his fight for the open Bible
against the opposition of priests, king, and nobles.

For about five hundred years there had been almost
a complete lull in the matter of Bible translation. The
Latin Vulgate was still fastened on the clergy and safely
kept from the common people. No great effort was made
to permit the people to have the Scriptures whether in
Latin or Anglo-Saxon. The Norman Conquest was three
hundred years old when Wycliffe began his work. As
we have seen, the Conquest brought in its trail the new
elements of the Norman-French into the family of the
Anglo-Saxon, which were in time to become unified both
as to blood and language. During this period all that
is strictly English was born. Here stands the English
Bible made by the hands of Wycliffe and his followers,

the Lollards, the poor priests who traveled in all parts of the country "calling men back to faith in the simple gospel of Christ."

Wycliffe's Bible stands as a great achievement in English Bible history. Produced sixty-eight years before the invention of the printing press, every line was written by hand. It was the first English Bible to mark chapter divisions in the several books of the Bible. It stands as one of the outstanding monuments of English literature. Of these Wycliffe Bibles there are about one hundred seventy copies in existence today, most of them being attributed to the successors of the great reformer. The reward that Wycliffe himself received for his consecrated work was bitterest persecution by the Church and clergy. Though dying a natural death, his body was taken from its burial place and publicly burned by order of the Pope; his ashes were thrown upon the river as a token of the "destruction of his memory." But the world would not have it so, for Wycliffe holds today his honored place among the heroic ancestors in our English Bible history.

II. TYNDALE'S VERSION (1525)

The century and a half following Wycliffe witnessed great changes in the world. It was the new era. The thoughts of the Western world began to turn to the culture of ancient Greece and Rome; interest was quickened in the perfection of their arts; literature came in for special consideration and with the revival of the classics of Homer, Sophocles, Horace, Vergil, and others of the old masters, new inspiration was given. Hand in hand with the rebirth of language studies, the Greek and Hebrew Scriptures came forth to produce a new era in Bible translation. The printing press was also within reach to multiply and spread the results of the scholars' work. Through the medium of the printed page the Bible was now to find its distribution on a worldwide scale.

When William Tyndale, a master in seven languages, began his labors in Bible translation, he had in his hands some of the old manuscripts of the Hebrew Old Testament and the Greek New Testament. Though these manuscripts were not as old as some more recently discovered, we find here the scholarly method of going back to original sources for translations into English.

Judged by highest standards of personality and scholarly ability Tyndale was the outstanding man of his day, and one of the greatest men in English history. In spite of his unusual preparation for his work, however, probably because of it, he was continually interrupted by terrible persecution by the Church, particularly by the bishop of London, who was his bitterest enemy. Finally driven into exile, he found refuge in the German cities of Hamburg, Cologne, and Worms. Here on foreign soil William Tyndale labored on his translations of the Hebrew and Greek Scriptures for the sake of his countrymen. In the city of Worms, the place to which Martin Luther (1521) was conducted for trial before the Diet of Worms, Tyndale completed his translation of the New Testament into English. Printed copies of this work were sent to England in large numbers, though their importation was forbidden by decree. Copies were smuggled in concealed in bales of merchandise and in other ways. In order that this English New Testament might not find its way into the hands of the people, Bishop Tunstall instructed his agents to purchase all copies that they could at any price. The proceeds from these sales, including the profits, were used in printing more New Testaments which were forwarded to England as rapidly as they could be produced. But the opposition to Tyndale increased. His work was eyed with suspicion and deep hatred. The great translator became the object of many conspiracies hatched out by his own countrymen. His betrayal by a trusted friend is one of the saddest stories in history, and his death by burning most pathetic. But his work was done and remained. The results of his labor reappeared in several versions of the English Bible, especially in Coverdale's Version and the King James.

For the right to read the Scriptures and for the opportunity of so doing, Tyndale made the supreme sacrifice. His interest in the common people became a passion. He is said to have answered a critical clergyman in the following manner: "If God spare my life, ere many years I shall cause a boy that driveth the plough shall know more of the Scriptures than thou dost." His last prayer for England and his countrymen was, "O Lord, open the King of England's eyes." How well both of those desires were fulfilled! We delight to think of Tyndale now as the father of our English Bible.

III. COVERDALE'S VERSION (1535)

In 1935 the Christian world closed a fitting celebration marking the four hundredth anniversary of the first complete Bible printed in the English language. That was the Bible of Miles Coverdale (1488-1569). Unlike John Wycliffe and William Tyndale, both of whom were rigid, rugged in character, impatient, and unyielding, Miles Coverdale was gentle in disposition and more moderate in his dealings. His mild manner created no bitter enemies, but enabled him to secure for his work the help of the ablest leaders of his day. In scholarly ability he was outstanding, but not equal to William Tyndale, the most highly educated man of his day. Coverdale's introduction to his own version of the English Bible sets forth in a most beautiful manner his humble spirit and great ambition for his people: "To say the truth before God, it was neither my labor nor desire to have this work put into my hand; nevertheless it grieved me that other nations should be more plenteously provided for with the scriptures in their mother tongue than we;

therefore when I was instantly required, though I could not do it as well as I would, I thought it yet my duty to do my best and that with a good will." In those words we can see a man of towering character and good will. Furthermore, we are told by Coverdale himself that his translation was not based on the original Scriptures of the Hebrew and Greek but that he relied on the versions of others, as follows: "Faithfully and truly translated out of the Douche (German) and Latyn into English." And, again: "I have with a clear conscience purely and faithfully translated out of five sundry interpreters, having only the manifest truths of the scriptures before my eyes."

Now, as shown in his introduction, Coverdale had before him the Latin and German versions of the Bible which he used in making his English translation. But these were not all. Special attention is called to the fact that the work of his predecessors, Wycliffe and Tyndale, was also in his hands. This was providential, for it was through Coverdale that the best of Tyndale was passed on to the future. To what extent he leaned on Wycliffe is not known. But, true to his fine sense of values and personal modesty, he took from others their great achievements and saved them for the future. Thus it came to pass that the work of William Tyndale, placed under the ban while he was living and bitterly condemned after his martyrdom, was received without question in the version by Miles Coverdale.

But we do not dismiss Coverdale simply with this statement. He was a genius of his own kind. For beauty of English, depth of expression, and sweetness of spirit, no one surpassed him. How poor we would be if Coverdale's voice were silenced! Indeed, some of the finest passages in the English Bible translation come directly from him. Because of this excellence in his language he will continue to speak. In greatness he stands with Wycliffe and Tyndale, equally honored and revered for his work's sake.

IV. THE GREAT BIBLE (1539)

In the line of descent of our English Bible, there are two versions which come between Coverdale's Bible and the Great Bible.[1] In view of the fact that they were mainly concerned with setting forward the fine results of preceding translations, we may omit them from further discussion. It is true that the Great Bible was also an attempted improvement of the work of Tyndale and Coverdale and that, in all probability, the Great Bible was largely the work of Coverdale himself. At any rate we know that it was Miles Coverdale who received permission to publish this Bible thus giving to it the distinction of being the only version ever authorized by a king of England. This was done, of course, during the reign of Henry VIII. The King James Version of 1611, known through the centuries as the Authorized Version, never received that standing by royal decrees. Prior to the Great Bible, all versions were permitted or perhaps commended but none actually authorized. In case of the Great Bible, its authorization immediately placed it in the front rank of English versions, a position it held for thirty years. It was placed by decree in every parish church in England, thus excluding all other versions. In 1546 there was an organized effort to destroy by fire every other version of the English Bible. As a result the attention of the people was directed to the Scriptures as never before, and it is probably to this era that we must assign that great renewal of interest in the Bible which followed.

V. THE GENEVA BIBLE (1560)

This version of the English Scriptures gets its name from the fact that it was made and published in Geneva,

---

[1]Reference is here made to *Matthew's Bible* which was published in 1537, and *Taverner's Bible* in 1539. These are not to be regarded as original works though each had some outstanding merits. Matthew's Bible was largely a revision of the work of Tyndale and Coverdale, while Taverner's was an attempted revision of Matthew's, especially in the New Testament. Thus the former versions were simply brought forward. This is largely true also of the Great Bible, but there are other reasons for calling special attention to it as the next step.

Switzerland. Unsettled political conditions in England following the reign of Henry VIII, especially the revival of Catholic power under Queen Mary, made it necessary for evangelical leaders and reformers to seek refuge in foreign lands. To Geneva they fled and there in earnest labor wrought out the best version of the English Bible that had yet appeared. In this work we find William Whittingham of Oxford leading, assisted by two of the greatest figures in religious reform, John Knox and John Calvin. In addition to these there is reason to believe that the gifted Coverdale made his contribution. In the immediate background of the Geneva Bible stands the monumental work of William Tyndale. Though running along with the Great Bible, which was now the Authorized Version of the Church of England, the Geneva Bible quickly won its way into the hearts of the people of England and Scotland. It was closely associated with the Puritan movement in England and thus widened its influence in popular regard. This position of favor was maintained by the Geneva Version for almost three quarters of a century, being displaced only by the Authorized Version of 1611.

VI. THE BISHOPS' BIBLE (1569)

As stated in a letter of Archbishop Cranmer to Cromwell, the secretary of state under Henry VIII, it is clear that the bishops of the Church were planning to enter the field of English Bible translation, as follows: "I pray you, my Lord, that you will exhibit the book (that is, Matthew's Bible) unto the King's highness, and to obtain of his grace, if you can, a license that the same may be sold and read of every person, without danger of any act, proclamation, or ordinance, heretofore granted to the contrary, *until such time that we bishops shall set forth a better translation*, which I think will not be till a day after doomsday." That was written 1536. Meanwhile Taverner's Bible had appeared (1539), the Great Bible (1539), and the Geneva Bible (1560), but the bishops had not attempted a better translation. Spurred on by the success of the reformers whose Geneva Bible was increasing in popular favor every year, the bishops began their work. It was intended, of course, that their Bible should displace both the Great Bible and the Geneva Bible. At this time, therefore, there were three prominent English versions struggling for popular support. Gradually the Great Bible lost its position because the bishops preferred their own translation in the churches. In the long run the two remaining versions, the Bishops' and the Geneva Bible, held the stage until the King James Version was made in 1611.

VII. THE ROMAN BIBLE (1582-1609)

As a general rule, not much attention is given to the Roman Bible in tracing English Bible history. We regard this, however, as a serious omission since it is concerned with a translation designed to meet the needs of millions of English speaking people who were largely dependent on the Latin Vulgate for their knowledge of the Scriptures. In a sense it was an effort on the part of the Roman Church to offset the advantages gained by the Church of England and evangelical bodies in England in making the Scriptures available to the people. In point of time the first part of the Roman Bible appeared in 1582. It consisted only of the New Testament, and was based altogether on the Latin Vulgate of Jerome. The authors of this work were, for the greater part, Catholic refugees from England. The name, The Rheims New Testament, is derived from the French city where the translation was made and printed. The second portion of the Roman Bible, the Douay Version of the Old Testament, was published at Douay, France, in 1609 and 1610, about thirty years after the New Testament. The whole work is referred to as the Douay Version and is the Bible for all English speaking Catholics. It contains, of course, all the books recognized by the Roman Church, including the Apocrypha, and to that extent radically differs from other English versions. In addition to that difference, moreover, the light of modern scholarship has not been allowed to play on the Douay Version with the result that it still contains the imperfections of the Vulgate.

VIII. THE KING JAMES VERSION (1611)

When King James was crowned ruler of England in 1603, there were three versions of the English Bible in circulation. Chief among these was the Geneva Bible, made by refugee Protestants in Switzerland, which gradually won its way as the favorite with the mass of English people; next was the Bishops' Bible which, because of its clerical backing, maintained an influential position; and, last, the Great Bible which had been authorized by the king in 1539 and which was still chained to the wooden desks of many country churches. It was clear, however, that none of these versions was to be regarded as final; each one could be greatly improved. Their defects were freely recognized and discussed; many scholars, consecrated and competent, were standing ready to offer their talents in unselfish service. King James, in common with other enlightened leaders of his realm, not only had grace to sense the need and the opportunity, but took practical steps to see that the work was done. The way in which he proceeded with the undertaking shows very plainly that he was anxious to present a Bible that would meet with popular approval. It was not to be a sectarian Bible, appealing to special classes or groups, but the common property of all. The men selected to do the work were not chosen because of their party or group relations, but solely because of scholarly ability. An examination of this circle of fifty-four scholars shows that some were churchmen, others were Puritan, and still others of no party at all. By the order of King James, and through royal support, these men were commissioned to do the work. The records of their meetings show that the work of translation was begun in 1607 and that, after years of earnest labor, it was completed, the results being given to the world in the King James Version of 1611.

On the title page of this version we have the following statement: "The Holy Bible, containing the Old and New Testaments; translated out of the original tongues; and with the former translations diligently compared and revised, by his majesty's special command. Appointed to be read in the churches." In this very interesting statement reference is made to several important points which call for fuller explanation. *First*, the King James Version, like Tyndale's Version, is based on the original tongues. By this is meant, of course, that the translators had before them the Hebrew and Greek Scriptures. We have already learned that all Hebrew manuscripts are practically the same and that the accepted text is the Massoretic. In the use of the Hebrew text, therefore, the translators were not under any very great disadvantages. With regard to the Greek Scriptures, however, they had no ancient manuscripts but based their work on the Greek cursives extending from the tenth to the fifteenth centuries. None of the great capital letter manuscripts was yet in use, some were not even discovered.[2] *Secondly*, the translators made use of former versions which gave them a basis for comparison and revision. We are not to understand that this reference to former versions includes only the English versions of Wycliffe, Tyndale, Coverdale, Geneva, etc., for in the dedication to the king the translators clearly state that they also used the versions of foreign languages for the sake of greater accuracy. Their statement is worthy of being quoted: "That out of the Original Sacred Tongues, together with comparing of the labours, both in our own, and other foreign languages, of the many worthy men who went before us, there should be one more exact Translation of the Holy Scriptures into the English Tongue." From this it is evident that the trans-

[2] See chapter 4, and note on page 86.

lators went to the current versions in English, French, German, etc., in order to produce a version of highest rank. *Thirdly,* it is further stated by the translators that their work was being done at the command of the king and under his direction. Because of royal connection the King James Version was "appointed to be read in the churches." This statement is also of great interest since it seems to suggest that the king formally approved the version as *authorized.* Accordingly, we have always referred to the King James Bible as the Authorized Version. There is no record that proves this, or any statement that it was the authorized version for the English people. As a matter of fact, Coverdale's Bible and Matthew's Bible were both formally authorized as to sale and circulation, but the only Bible ever authorized to the exclusion of others was the Great Bible of 1539. Since then no other Bible has been definitely set up as authorized by any king of England.

It is even now generally recognized that the King James Version is the most popular Bible among English speaking people everywhere. For beauty and simplicity of language, and for depth of spirit, it has no equal, nor even a close second. During recent years the splendid revised versions have appeared, but it is a fact that they have not even threatened to displace the version of 1611. Of course the old order always passes slowly, and many students of the Bible think that it is only a question of time when the King James Bible will lose its sway. That remains to be seen, of course, but at present it seems very doubtful. As it now stands, this version of the Bible is one of the really great monuments of the English language. By virtue of its reproduction of the truth and spirit of the Scriptures in the purest words of our English tongue, it deserves its continued mission of unsurpassed usefulness.

IX. The Revised Version (1885)

The King James Version was given to the English people in 1611. After a short period, in which a few changes were made in the interest of clearness, it quickly established itself as the most popular Bible in the kingdom. Immediately following its publication, conditions in England became very unsettled. No more serious attempts were made in the matter of Bible translations. The result was that the King James was left with no rival in the field. The passing years served to establish it more securely in the affections of the people.

From 1611 to 1885, that is from the King James to the Revised Version, represents a period of two and three-quarter centuries. During that period several important developments took place, each one centering the attention on the need for improvement in the English Bible. *First,* the language itself was undergoing changes. Words formerly used were either discarded or, remaining, were liable to be misunderstood. More than two hundred and fifty words had lost their original meaning in English. In addition new words were being formed to express more exactly the thought of the people. That process continues today, as every student knows. *Secondly,* scholarship was becoming more exacting and more determined to reproduce as far as possible the thoughts of the writers in the Scriptures. Of equal importance was the fact that the scholars themselves were advanced in their mastery of the ancient languages, particularly the Hebrew and the Greek. *Thirdly,* during this period occurred some of the most remarkable discoveries in Bible history—the finding of the great manuscripts of the Bible, some of them going back to the very threshold of the first Christian century. Not one of these capital letter manuscripts had ever been used in former revisions. They demanded, accordingly, that revision of the Bible be made in the light of the earliest texts. And, *finally,* with the discovery of these new materials (and thousands of other manuscripts and written sources in

addition) the science of textual criticism took the field
in the interest of exactness in Bible translation. The
purpose of this science is, first of all, to restore the original language of the Bible records as nearly as possible.
That work has been crowned with remarkable success.

The Revised Version of the Scriptures is the work of
enlightened and consecrated scholarship, and represents
one of the finest achievements in English Bible translation. It is the product of learned and devout men of
different religious groups who labored in this work of
love for ten years. The Version is absolutely free from
bias and prejudice of any kind and secures fairness for
all in the translation of the Scriptures. As already
pointed out, it rests on the oldest manuscripts available.
Its text is the most perfect that we have yet received
and its language conveys the true sense of the Scriptures
in a wonderful manner. The New Testament Version
was completed in 1881 and the Old Testament in 1884.
One year later, 1885, both were published under the
title the Revised Version.

Though the Revised Version marks the highest point
yet reached by scholarship in English Bible history, the
public has not shown any great enthusiasm in accepting
the results. As already stated, this lack of enthusiasm
might be explained on the ground that old things pass
very slowly, and that in time the Revised Version will be
recognized at its true worth. At any rate, everyone
understands that the final word in English Bible translation has not yet been spoken, and probably never will
be. Even at this present hour Bible scholars both in
England and the United States are laboring on an improvement in this outstanding work. The process is
slow and great expense is involved but progress is noted
everywhere. We rejoice in all of this toil of consecrated
men whose chief ambition is to let the Word of God
say in English everything that it says so clearly and
so powerfully in the Hebrew Old Testament and the
Greek New Testament.

X. The American Standard Version (1901)

The years that witnessed the labors of English Bible scholars in making the Revised Version saw also a constant interchanging of views with American scholars in regard to acceptable and advisable changes in the current King James Version. The most friendly relations existed between these two groups in their common work. It was agreed that all changes made in the biblical text should be allowed to run for fourteen years, but that at the end of that period the changes suggested by the American scholars might be included in an American edition of the Revised Version. In 1901 this edition appeared under the name of the American Standard Version. The same earnest labor was expended on this version as on the Revised, the results being highly satisfactory. The chief difference between the Revised and the American Standard is in the rendering of certain passages where American opinion was preferred to that of the English. The American Standard has many points of excellence and it is gradually finding an enlarged place in popular approval.

XI. The Revised Standard Version (1946 and 1952)

In 1937 a comprehensive revision of the American Standard Version was undertaken by a group of scholars appointed by the International Council of Religious Education. The committee worked diligently in two sections, one dealing with the Old Testament and one with the New Testament. In 1945 the committee working on the New Testament completed its work, and the Revised Standard Version was published early in 1946. The work on the Old Testament was completed in 1952 and the Revised Standard Version of the entire Bible was published at that time.

XII. Modern Translations

While modern translations of the Bible are not to be regarded as making any serious effort to displace the more popular versions now in use, they represent a phase of English Bible history that should not be overlooked. As a matter of fact, they have never attained popularity and probably never will. They vary considerably in value. In quality of translation they range from the literal and scholarly to the free and loose, these latter being more of the nature of paraphrases than translations. The best work in this aspect of Bible translation is probably that of Moffatt's, though excellent translations have been produced by Weymouth, Goodspeed, and others. As suggested above, though the value of these translations or paraphrases from the standpoint of the average reader of the Bible might be great, there is no indication that they will ever be in general use. The standard versions which have held the field through the centuries will continue, with periodic revisions, to meet the popular approval, use, and demand.

QUESTIONS FOR REVIEW

1. Name the factors that have greatly influenced the course of English Bible history from the Norman conquest to the modern age.
2. Describe the work of John Wycliffe.
3. Discuss the labors of William Tyndale.
4. What were the sources of Miles Coverdale's translation of the Scriptures? Did Coverdale depend on Tyndale's work?
5. What was the only version of the Bible ever authorized by a king of England?
6. Who were the authors of the Geneva Bible?
7. What was the purpose of the bishops in making their version of the Bible?
8. What is the Bible for English speaking Catholics?
9. Describe the King James Version.
10. Give an estimate of the Revised Version.
11. What is the difference between the Revised Version and the American Standard Version?
12. What is the value of modern translations?

PRESENT POSITION OF THE BIBLE

OUTLINE

INTRODUCTORY

I. IN THE LIFE OF MANKIND

II. IN THE WORK OF THE CHURCHES

1. The Glory of the Churches
2. Faithful Observance of the Ordinances
3. Evangelism in the Churches
4. Missions in the Churches
5. Progressive and Confident in Labor

III. IN SCIENTIFIC INVESTIGATION, ILLUSTRATIONS SHOWING RESULTS OF MODERN RESEARCH

1. The Career of Abraham
2. Evidences of the Flood
3. The People Called Hittites
4. The Exodus from Egypt
5. Destruction of Jericho
6. The Temple in Jerusalem
7. Bethlehem of Judea
8. Nazareth in Galilee
9. The Well of Jacob
10. The Synagogue at Capernaum

IV. IN STUDENT CIRCLES

PRESENT POSITION OF THE BIBLE

INTRODUCTORY

In closing our survey of English Bible history it will not be out of order to call attention to some special points with which the student should be reasonably familiar. The Bible occupies such a commanding position in modern thought that we cannot afford to lag behind in the earnest effort to see clearly its values and to defend it on the basis of its abiding worth. In doing this it is not necessary, nor desirable, that we take an offensive attitude toward any and all questions raised about the Bible as the Word of God to the world, nor to refuse to accept all the real light that scholarship can throw on its wonderful history and its deeper meaning. At no time, whether ancient or modern, has God placed a premium on ignorance; we should continue to believe in fullest measure that he wants us to know as much as it is possible for us to know and to apply ourselves constantly to problems of knowledge. Furthermore, we may confidently believe that God approves the humble and serious approach to the Book of all books to find its deeper and truer interpretation under the leadership of the Holy Spirit whom he promised: "When he, the Spirit of truth, is come, he shall guide you into all the truth: . . . he shall take of mine, and shall declare it unto you."[1] In no other way do we seek to know the full meaning of the Bible or its great significance for men of all ages and, especially, the modern age.

Nor has God left us without many marks of his divine favor on the Bible both as to its wonderful history and its abiding truthfulness. New chapters in that story of

[1] John 16:13-14.

God's approval are being continually written, always with the result that the Bible grows dearer and stronger and the circle of its sacred influence is enlarged. Of course it has always been the Great Book of the ages, but none would question the statement that today the Bible is greater in the thoughts of men than ever in the history of the world. We take that to be one of the evidences of its divine mission and purpose. In the following summary we present four considerations that should cause every lover of the Bible to rejoice and to be grateful. These facts command attention while giving assurance that the future of Bible study will probably be the brightest that we have yet experienced. The devotion of our young people to biblical interests already justifies that confident expectation. Well, it must be that way for us; the Bible remains our chart and compass and so long as *we remain with it* we need fear no departure from our proper course as a people.

I. In the Life of Mankind

In calling attention to some of the outstanding facts connected with the present position of the Bible, the first to be considered is its unique relation to the life of mankind. American and English students of this generation are fully acquainted with the great influence of the Bible on every aspect of Western civilization and, particularly, with its contribution to the high ideals of life in their own countries. In the development of home, church, and state the Word of God has been at the very foundation of our progress and has determined the general lines of our advance. It would probably be in full keeping with the facts to speak of ourselves as a people of one Book. Through the centuries there has been the powerful influence of the Scriptures that has determined the standards and ideals of life as we understand and pursue them. The results have been seen in national policies and in our world relations. The tone that the Bible has given to all of our dealings has been of the noblest quality, and this in turn has commanded respect in all quarters of the world.

But the influence of the Bible on English-speaking peoples is only one phase of its world mission. This great Book is not the product of American or English scholarship nor is it the result of scholarly work on the part of any other people however enlightened and consecrated. Though made *for* man and *with* man under the direction of the Spirit, it is not a human product. It is designed for all men and is of sacred importance to every nation, but these facts do not grow out of any human origins; fundamentally they themselves are based on God's purpose and answer in meeting human needs. In simplest terms the needs of all men, regardless of race, station, color, or clime are the same, because all have sinned and come short of the glory of God. Since God is no respecter of persons; that is, since God is not partial in the expression of his love and grace, the offer of salvation to every man is a matter of urgent necessity. The gospel message as recorded in the Bible is of prime importance to Asiatics, Europeans, Americans, and others, but it is not of more importance to one than it is to another. The need of salvation is not fixed by boundaries or provinces, nor can the answer of that need as proclaimed in the Bible be confined to any one section of the world.

With the spread of the Bible during the past four hundred years we have seen a new Pentecost in the experience of the nations when practically all men have heard the Good News in their own languages. This modern gift of tongues has been made possible through the printed word which now holds out a Bible, or portions of the Bible, to widely separated tribes and races who speak in almost a thousand languages. The most recent achievement is the labor of a missionary through six years to form a written language whereby the New Testament could be placed in the hands of 450,000 Siamese. That work is going on all the time. All languages are being placed under tribute to give expression to the love of God and to make available for all the records of his redeeming work through the centuries.

With the removal of the barriers of language the Bible now speaks around the world its message of life, love, and liberty. The waiting hearts of men receive the glad tidings with great joy. The Book of God is at home wherever introduced. Transformation of life and conditions begins immediately to be seen and felt; the upreach, desires, goals, and ideals are shaped by the presence of the Bible. As this leaven of truth and righteousness works in every phase of human thought and conditions, it makes more real the abundant life in Christ. There is no need for us to think of this result as marvelous or unusual; it is simply the fulfilment of the mission of the Bible. The hand of God is clearly in this world reception of the Word of God. And, finally, as the presence of the Book in our midst has been attended by wondrous results in every sphere of our life, so will it produce similar results in the life of men anywhere.

II. IN THE WORK OF THE CHURCHES

The present position of the Bible in the work of the churches calls for attention and emphasis. It should never become necessary for anyone in our ranks to start a "Back to the Bible Movement," for we should never think for a moment that we could leave it and still prosper. As churches and as a denomination we must refuse to stand by anything that cannot be supported in principle by the Bible, nor fail to do that which is plainly commanded and urged. If our work in the kingdom of God is vital and genuine, as we believe it is, we can well afford to let the revealed Word of God cast upon it a constant play of light. That is to say, we should take the Bible seriously and reverently as the final authority in what we believe and do, also in what we propose to do. But in order to carry out this program of service based on the Bible, it is clear that the Bible must occupy its proper place in all of our thought and purpose. We pause here to present the following phases of our work which always should be seen in the full light of the Word of God.

1. *The Glory of the Churches*

The Bible makes it perfectly clear that the business of extending the kingdom of God rests on the churches. The New Testament view of the churches is that each one of them is a spiritual democracy, composed of baptized believers, redeemed by the blood of Christ, observing the ordinances, working together for the triumph of principles of righteousness and truth, and seeking to bring the message of redemption to the heart of every man. As a spiritual body concerned with spiritual business, it is the greatest institution in the world. We believe that it should be completely separated from political bodies, and that in the carrying out of its spiritual mission the church should receive no support from the state. We hold, furthermore, that as the representatives of Christ, the churches should be beyond reproach and positively engaged in rebuilding society on the basis of redeemed individuals. This is the supreme business of the churches and the doing of this work is their chief glory.

2. *Faithful Observance of the Ordinances*

It is significant that Jesus never laid on his followers the obligation to observe numerous ordinances. He commanded only two and both were chosen primarily to set forth the personal relations of the believer with his Lord. For us, therefore, the ordinances of baptism and the Lord's Supper are of first importance and should be carried out faithfully by every follower of Jesus. In baptism the believer shows forth his death and resurrection to a new life in the likeness of the death, burial, and resurrection of Jesus, while in the Lord's Supper there is a continual setting forth of his fellowship with Jesus and the confident expectation of his second coming. These are vital matters. The Bible teaching is clear on these points, and every Christian should seek to carry them out faithfully in full keeping with New Testament requirements. These ordinances are marked by high privilege, and their proper observance will issue in great blessings.

3. *Evangelism in the Churches*

When viewed in the light of the great system of priesthood, sacrifices, and ritual of the Old Testament, the churches of the New Testament appear in almost rugged simplicity. They do not seem to have been much concerned about a good many of the external features of church life to which we now give great attention. Of course conditions have changed and we think that our ways of doing the work can be justified. That is probably true. But we cannot justify any phase of our present work except in the light of its vital relation to our principal business, that is, evangelism. The whole business of the churches is to proclaim the gospel and to bring its message to bear on every heart. The early disciples began to herald the gospel in the local community and continued step by step in an onward and outward movement. The spirit of evangelism was strong and genuine. The blessings of God were showered on these first century Christians; thousands were added to the churches as the message was preached. It is necessary for us to recapture this fervent evangelism and to allow it full range in our Christian zeal to win others. Of course we must do other things, also, but if we do not evangelize it will not be necessary to do anything else. We justify the existence of the churches in winning the lost.

4. *Missions in the Churches*

The Bible is a missionary book. It is the living record of God's unceasing activity in the cause of missions.

We can never understand the Bible unless we read it as
a message from the heart of God to the world. The
business of missions, though carried on in the present
framework of time and space, is no product of time nor
of space. The Scriptures state that it is the expression
of the eternal purpose of God who offered up his Son
as a sacrifice for sin from the foundation of the world.[2]
With the fall of man the purpose of God swings into
action on the plane of human history. In the Old
Testament we have the story of the choice of Abraham
and of Israel for a world mission and a world blessing.
The prophets catch the meaning of the divine plan and,
through the Spirit of God, throw on the screen of the
world's night of sin and despair the promise of salvation
in the coming Messiah. The nations come up to Mt.
Zion to share in its love, its light, and law, while Israel
is pictured as on a mission of spiritual blessing to the
nations. The great climax of this divine movement was
reached in Bethlehem of Judea when Jesus was born.
How wonderful was the angel's announcement to the
shepherds! "Be not afraid; for behold, I bring you
good tidings of great joy which shall be to all the people:
for there is born to you this day in the city of David
a Saviour, who is Christ the Lord."[3] The wonder of
that announcement still grips our hearts.

But Bethlehem was not an afterthought with God; it
was his forethought, forever fixed at the center of his
purposes of grace. And that is where it is today. We
sense the real message of the Bible only when we see in
it Jesus, the Son of God and the Saviour of men. The
first requirement for understanding Jesus is to see him
at the heart of missions. The whole business of missions is concerned with him from beginning to end and
if we are to have his fellowship we also must be concerned with missions from beginning to end. We could
never have received salvation apart from the mission

[2]Heb. 9:14; 1 Peter 1:19-20.
[3]Luke 2:10-11.

cause supported by others, nor could we have a greater mission than continuing that cause for the sake of others.

In regard to missions, therefore, the position of the Bible in the churches should never be thought of as secondary, but always recognized as vital to all missionary effort. Indeed, the biblical teaching on missions is fundamental in all activities of the churches as well as in the life of every Christian. To take "do nothing" and make a religion out of it is to commit spiritual suicide. The rekindling of the mission fires both at home and abroad will result in burning out the dross of selfishness and in restoring the pure metal of earnest zeal to share with all men the Good News of the kingdom of God. The plain message of the open Book is first and last the business of missions; the presence of antimissions or omissions is the fruit of an *unknown* Bible. The Word of God is perfectly clear on the work of the Christian. As the prism reflects clearly the seven colors of every ray of light, so does the receptive heart reflect the missionary ideals and goals of the Light of the World.

5. *Progressive and Confident in Labor*

Finally, the present position of the Bible in the churches serves to keep before the Christian heart the certain triumph of the Christian cause. A considerable portion of the Bible, both of the Old Testament and the New, was written to assure the people of God that the kingdom of God would prevail. Since the cause of truth and righteousness has always met with obstacles and difficulties, struggles and persecutions, the word of comfort, good cheer, promise, and assurance has ever been needed. In the present day the need is just as urgent, nor does the Bible fail to produce confidence regarding the final triumph of the cause of Christ. The note of victory is as clear as a bell. Jesus never failed to encourage the early disciples in their work though he never set any limit for spiritual triumph. He stressed rather constancy, loyalty, and faithfulness in labor. He urged

them to be progressive in spirit and assured them that
the strongholds of evil would not be able to stand against
their attack. It is plain that the apostles shared this
conviction with Jesus and urged it on the early Christians
and churches. In the book of the Revelation the final
scenes set forth the last stages of the great struggle between the forces of good and evil, leading up to the
appearance of the new heaven and the new earth wherein
dwell righteousness and peace.

Now the Bible stands as a constant reminder of this
ongoing and victorious movement, and in the light of
its clear teaching we may always find courage. The
churches should derive from the Word of God unfailing
instruction regarding not only the work to be done but
deep conviction that it cannot be undone. Paul's feeling about the matter is expressed as follows: "Where-
fore, my beloved brethren, be ye stedfast, unmovable,
always abounding in the work of the Lord, forasmuch
as ye know that your labor is not vain in the Lord."[4]

III. In Scientific Investigation

Modern scholarship has practically succeeded in rebuilding for us the world into which Christianity came.
Archeology, that is, "the science of old things," has
done special service. It is helping us now to understand
largely the conditions under which Jesus and the disciples lived in the first century and is giving us a close-up
of the world in which they labored. But far beyond the
days of the first Christian century, we can go with ease
into the early dawn of civilization in Egypt, Canaan,
and Mesopotamia, catching here and there glimpses of
the Patriarchs of Israel and patriarchs of other peoples
who lived many hundreds of years before Abraham,
Isaac, Jacob, and Moses. The kings of Israel and Judah,
the prophets of the Old Testament take their places in
the active life of their own age in close contact with
all surrounding nations. The story is a thrilling narra-

[4] 1 Cor. 15: 58.

tive of how men lived in the yesterdays of the world's history, just the same kind of story that we find in the books of the Old and New Testaments.

One of the most important facts for the student to keep in mind is that the Bible is an Oriental book written in the language and thought forms of the East.   To understand its thought and its word pictures we must stand in the place of the Orientals.   That is another way of saying that we have to know the historical, geographical, social, political, and religious backgrounds of the Bible in order to understand the Bible.   It is just at that point that scientific help is being given to us at present.   It is now possible to reproduce the actual conditions under which the great characters of the Bible lived and worked, to get a closer view of the daily affairs in which they were engaged, and, out of this fuller knowledge, to understand better the messages which they gave to the world.   Though much has been learned, we are merely in the beginning of larger knowledge and fuller understanding.   If one should ask, In what way has the Bible been aided by scientific or scholarly work? the answer would require books instead of pages.   It is clear, however, that this is a question of great interest and that some of the results of modern research should be presented at this point. The following illustrations will not be without value in showing the truthfulness and accuracy of the Bible.   We select five examples from the Old Testament and five from the New Testament.

1. The Career of Abraham

The Old Testament account of the life of Abraham grows more fascinating every year.   With the progress of excavation in the Near and Middle East we are able to see the conditions under which this great man lived and to follow him step by step from his native land to the Land of Promise.   Special attention is here called to Ur of the Chaldees, the city of his birth.   It was one of the oldest cities of the Middle East, situated near the

Euphrates River as it entered the Persian Gulf. Investigations at Ur show that the city was about seven miles in circumference, and protected by great walls. The city was planned with principal streets, some running at right angles as in our modern towns. We know the type of dwellings occupied by citizens of Ur. The city had schools, banks, and temples. The main center of worship, the great Ziggurat in the heart of the city, still stands. We know something of the trades followed by these people, the goldsmith being of special prominence because of his fine work. Excavations are being continued at this wonderful place. From Ur of the Chaldees Abraham followed the great highway into the land of Canaan and down into Egypt. At every point the Bible story is being illustrated and confirmed in what it has to say of Abraham and his career.

2. *Evidences of the Flood*

The early chapters of Genesis have long been under the searching eyes of the critics. Particular attention has been given to the account of the flood. In spite of the fact that earlier peoples in Mesopotamia had their own accounts of the flood, some of which have been recovered dating back to about 2000 B.C., there was no serious disposition to think of these as reliable or true accounts of actual events. The flood was regarded as mythology or legend. The Bible account was included, also, and made to depend on the legends of other people taken over by the Hebrews. But this negative estimate of the flood account in Genesis has not been allowed to stand. The astounding results of excavations in Mesopotamia confirm the Bible story. According to C. Leonard Woolley the excavations at Ur show a mud deposit eight feet deep, lying between an older civilization and a later, that proves the correctness of the flood in this region. In other sections of Mesopotamia similar deposits of mud point to the correctness of the Bible story. Thus, step by step, the Bible is receiving support with the progress of research in Bible lands.

3. The People Called Hittites

Another illustration of the way in which scientific investigation has come to the support of the Bible is found in the strange people called Hittites. They are mentioned more than forty times in the records of the Old Testament. In view of the fact that no other ancient records mentioned them, the Old Testament accounts were regarded as legendary. It was thought that a people of such prominence as the Hittites could not have escaped the notice of ancient historians and records. Indeed, it was bluntly said that the Hittites never existed. But that conclusion on the part of the critics of the Bible has not been allowed to stand. Through excavations in Asia Minor, in the vicinity of the present capital of Turkey, the civilization of the ancient Hittites has come to light. We now know that they were among the three most important peoples of the world about 2000-1400 B.C., and that they occupied a vast area stretching from Asia Minor to Palestine. This is one of the thrilling stories of modern research. The Bible accounts have been found altogether accurate and reliable in what they say concerning the mysterious Hittites and their neighbors.

4. The Exodus from Egypt

The thrilling story of Israel's exodus from the land of Egypt and their arrival in the land of Canaan never loses its charm. The records of these events come to us from the earliest days of Israel's history and have always been accepted as true and thoroughly reliable. During recent years the Bible has been wonderfully supported by investigation on the part of scholars so that now we are able to reconstruct in large measure the stirring events of this period. It seems fairly certain that the exodus took place about 1445 B.C., that the great Pharaoh of the oppression was Thutmosis III, and the Pharaoh of the exodus, Amenhotep IV. It is highly probable that we can identify the daughter of Pharaoh who adopted Moses as her child. New light has been shed

on conditions in Canaan during this period in the
Amarna Letters which speak of the Hebrews invading
Canaan. It is widely held that these are the incoming
people of Israel under Joshua. It is perfectly marvelous
how the biblical records are receiving fresh support from
the monuments of the ancient world. The future bids
fair to place in our hands more startling results.

5. *Destruction of Jericho*

The last example of modern support of Old Testament
history and events is the fall of the great Canaanite
city of Jericho. The destruction of the city occurred at
the very beginning of the conquest of Canaan under
Joshua. All of us have been familiar with the details
of the siege of Jericho, including the silent march of
the Israelites around its walls for six days and the fall
of the ramparts on the seventh. The date of this event
has been fixed at about 1400 B.C. Through modern
investigation the old site of Jericho has been excavated
with the result that the details of its capture as given in
the Bible have been confirmed. One may stand on the
actual site of these stirring events and look at the brick
and stone walls that challenged the besieging Israelites.
We are not here concerned with the details but only with
the bare statement of modern research confirming the
biblical narratives.

6. *The Temple in Jerusalem*

In the city of Jerusalem stands Mount Moriah, the
place to which Abraham came to offer up his son Isaac.
In later years David purchased the top of this hill from
Araunah, the Jebusite, and set it apart as the holy place
for the Temple. Here Solomon built the magnificent
Temple which stood for almost four hundred years as
the religious center of Israel. The Temple was destroyed
by Nebuchadnezzar in 587 B.C., but was rebuilt by the
returning exiles under Zerubbabel. Completed in 516
B.C., this second Temple stood until Herod the Great

began to erect the wonderful Temple that was called by his own name. This last Temple was commenced in 19 B.C. and completed in A.D. 64. During the ministry of Jesus it was still in the process of construction, forty-six years of the building program having passed. When Herod's Temple was destroyed in A.D. 70 Jerusalem itself was levelled to the earth and the Jews driven out. All of these details connected with the Temple have been set forth in clear light through modern research. We are now able to follow step by step the great events that occurred in this sacred place in Jerusalem, the city of the great King.

7. *Bethlehem of Judea*

Bethlehem is one of the most interesting towns in Palestine. Its history reaches back into the early days before the children of Israel came into the land of Canaan. At the entrance into this little town Rachel, the wife of the patriarch Jacob, died when Benjamin was born. Her tomb is supposed to stand on the exact spot today. Bethlehem was the home of Naomi and Boaz, later of Ruth. Here lived Obed, and Jesse, the father of David. In later years it was called the city of David, the place where Jesus was born. The modern town of Bethlehem stands on the ancient site of the city looking down on the field of the shepherds where angels sang of the newborn King. Within the city proper stands the Church of the Nativity, erected by Constantine about A.D. 325 over the supposed cave where Jesus was born. Here one may come and stand at the very center of events that have vitally affected the history of the world. The story of the city of Bethlehem is now known and confirmed even in its details. In common with other biblical cities it is being made to stand out more clearly in the light of modern research.

8. *Nazareth in Galilee*

The present town of Nazareth stands on the site of the New Testament city where Jesus lived from the time

of the return from Egypt until he was about thirty
years of age. Altogether the Saviour lived here about
twenty-five years. The city stands in the uplands of
lower Galilee commanding a beautiful view of plains,
mountains, and seashore. By its door went the great
trade routes connecting east and west. Exposed to the
influence of Romans, Greeks, and neighboring peoples,
Nazareth, in common with other Galilean towns, was
more open and liberal than Jewish cities in the Southern
part of Palestine. It did not have the best reputation
in the days of Jesus, as suggested in the reply of Nathan-
ael, "Can any good thing come out of Nazareth?" Here
Jesus lived until his manifestation to Israel. There is no
question regarding the site nor its importance during the
days of the Master. Today Nazareth has a population
of over ten thousand people and is, of course, the point
of interest for every pilgrim to the land of our Lord.
From what we now know of the city we can allow it
great influence in the life of Jesus as he looked out from
its narrow streets on the busy world that continually
passed by flowing from east to west.

9. *The Well of Jacob*

In the early ministry of Jesus the well of Jacob
marked a turning point in relations between Jews and
Samaritans. The conversation of Jesus with the woman
of Samaria took place on this spot. The well itself goes
back to the days of the patriarch Jacob who made it
for his people and his cattle, finally giving the whole of
the territory to his son Joseph. Located in a beautiful
plain, under the shadows of the sacred mountains, Ebal
and Gerizim, it stood at the entrance to old Shechem
and on the main highway from Jerusalem to the north.
The setting is in full keeping with the events recorded in
the fourth chapter of John. This is one of the certain
sites associated with the ministry of Jesus. The well was
originally 115 feet deep, though the debris of the ages
has taken away something of its depth in the modern

period. It is now about eighty-five feet deep. One can stand here and get the vision that came both to the Samaritan woman and the disciples of Jesus as he spoke to all about the things of God. Indeed, the pilgrim cannot but feel that here, the place where he stands, is holy ground and that he is actually pausing in the steps of the Master.

10. *The Synagogue at Capernaum*

Modern investigation has practically restored for us not only the city of Capernaum, which had been lost for centuries, but the synagogue where Jesus preached the sermon on the Bread of life that came down from heaven. As an important center of Jewish life in Galilee, the city of Capernaum maintained a certain leadership both in commercial and political relations. It was certainly important as a religious center as shown by the splendid synagogue that is now being uncovered and rebuilt. In all probability this is the house of worship that was given by the Roman centurion to the Jews. Only a few years ago Capernaum, together with its doomed sister cities, Bethsaida and Chorazin, was not even located. The prophecy of Jesus regarding their destruction had been literally fulfilled. Today, through faithful and effective research, Capernaum is gradually coming to the surface and with it new light on some of the stirring events of the ministry of the Saviour.

IV. IN STUDENT CIRCLES

In our final statement regarding the present position of the Bible it is our purpose to center attention on the student approach and interest. The present generation of students of the Bible are fully alert to the significance of scholarly research and scientific investigation and are showing an increasing interest in relating the new knowledge to a fuller understanding of the Bible. Never in the history of our churches has there been such interest in Bible study as is witnessed today when thousands of young people are taking up the Scriptures for serious

examination of their content and purpose. This is one
of the most encouraging aspects of our whole denominational life. Paul did not hesitate to lay on the heart of
one of his young students the following counsel: "Give
diligence to present thyself approved unto God, a workman that needeth not to be ashamed, handling aright
the word of truth."[5] We believe that, were the apostle
here today to make a general survey of the position of
the Bible in the life of this generation of students, he
would thank God and take courage. Indeed, the bright-
ness of the outlook argues well for the future of our
work in the kingdom of God. We may expect better
prepared leaders to take up the positions of responsibility in our midst. Hand in hand with an instructed and
enlightened leadership the rank and file of our great
people will show an enlarged vision of denominational
mission and increasing usefulness. Thus a Bible-cen-
tered people will maintain sound instruction and work,
nor be bothered by the various "isms" that might defeat
both our mission and our message.

In saying that we ought to be a Bible centered people
we do not mean that we should merely emphasize or
feature the Bible in our study courses and in the other
aspects of church life, but that we should recognize in
fullest measure its divine power and authority. If it
has any right to speak, its counsel should be reverenced
and obeyed. And, by examination of its sacred content,
we will see that not only does it have a right to set up
its standards, but that in every sphere of our Christian
activity it is able to provide direction and dynamic.
Anything that is of interest to God and man is regarded
by the Bible as fundamentally important. It lays down
its principles and sets up its goals in church, state, and
home; in social and religious interests, in economic and
political spheres, it has its own message for the people
of God. The Bible touches a man at every point of his
interests respecting God and his fellow men; it influences

---

[5] 2 Tim. 2:15.

in a definite and powerful way everything and everyone
that it touches. This fact is a proof of its divine mission.
The point here emphasized, however, does not refer in
the first instance to the great influence of the Bible, but
to the obligation on the part of students of the Bible to
be familiar with the book that produces such results.

Indeed we believe that instruction in the Bible should
be a vital part of our educational processes. Every student should have an intelligent appreciation of the history, content, and mission of the greatest Book in the
world. For if education is concerned chiefly with preparation *for life*, here is the Book that tells what life is at
its best and highest, and what should be its great con-
cerns, ideals, and goals. The possession of this kind of
knowledge is not only commended but commanded. To
be well grounded in the Bible, to be familiar with its
standards and its values, is to have not only an abiding
safeguard against all forms of godless education, but a
real power for high accomplishments. Low conceptions
of life and false standards of living can never flourish
where the Bible is allowed to shed its own light and to
set up its own ideals.

Regarded from the standpoint of denominational outlook and mission, the present generation of young people,
thoroughly instructed in the Bible, will be in a position
to render far-reaching service. By this we mean that
there will be an increasing spirit of co-operation in common interests both abroad and at home, and that the
approach to our tasks and privileges will be made with
clearer understanding and deeper sympathy. An illu-
mined mind is not only the work of the Holy Spirit, it is
also his chief ally; an understanding heart never allows
the spirit of antimissions to go unchallenged. Our
young people have sensed the real need of the hour and
by their serious and sustained interest in Bible study will
naturally forge ahead in prepared leadership and service.
Sooner or later we must see to it that all of our work
must be placed on real knowledge of the Bible which

is its abiding foundation. For, among all people of the world, we can least afford to be deficient in or ignorant of the Scriptures. In a democracy of believers we must continue to put great stress on the spiritual preparation and mental equipment of the individual. Our advance and progress will always be along the highway of truth revealed, studied, and understood.

And, finally, the present generation of Bible students will be tomorrow's defenders and interpreters of the faith. They will have to fight the intellectual and spiritual battles of Christianity. Frankly, we must recognize that this is not something that they may or may not do; it is not a question of permission but of absolute necessity. None will be in a position to interpret or defend the Word of God who does not know it; and he who knows it will never be slow to champion its cause. To every age it will come with renewed power and appeal, offering in Christ the full and final answer to every question relating to God and men. In our hands it is OUR BIBLE, our sacred heritage. May it always hold its position of pre-eminence in our affections and in our labors.

QUESTIONS FOR REVIEW

1. Discuss the Bible in relation to mankind.
2. What is the relation of the Bible to our denominational beliefs and work? Name the five phases of our work which should always be seen in the light of the Bible.
3. In what way has scientific investigation contributed to Bible study?
4. Describe each of the ten illustrations given to throw light on the Scriptures.
5. What is the present attitude of students toward the new knowledge?
6. What is meant by being a Bible centered people?
7. What is the special value of the Bible in the matter of life's goals and ideals?
8. In what way are students of today related to the future of the Bible and Bible study?

QUESTIONS FOR REVIEW AND EXAMINATION

QUESTIONS FOR REVIEW AND EXAMINATION

For instructions concerning the examination and the requesting of awards see Directions for the Teaching and the Study of This Book for Credit, page xi.

CHAPTER I

1. What is the first requirement for Bible study?
2. Define revelation. What is meant by self-revelation?
3. What are the two conditions under which revelation must take place?
4. Why is revelation confined to the plane of history?
5. Discuss the Bible as the record of revelation.

CHAPTER II

6. What is meant by the "upward slope" from the Old Testament to the New?
7. How would you define inspiration?
8. What is the meaning of 2 Timothy 3:16?
9. Explain 2 Peter 1:19-21.
10. Name four modern theories of inspiration, giving their chief characteristics.

CHAPTER III

11. Explain the origin of the word "Bible."
12. What is the meaning of the term "Canon"?
13. Name the divisions of the Old Testament according to the Hebrew classification. What is the English Bible arrangement of Old Testament books?
14. Explain how the sacred writings of the Hebrews were preserved through the centuries.
15. What are the divisions of the New Testament?
16. Name the earliest portions of the New Testament. What is the chronological order of all the New Testament books?
17. Discuss the formation of the New Testament Canon.

Chapter IV

18. What is the meaning of the term "manuscript"? What is an autograph?

19. Discuss the principal work of the Hebrew scribes.

20. Why are there so few manuscripts of the Old Testament?

21. What is the difference between an *uncial* manuscript and a *cursive* manuscript?

22. Name the six principal manuscripts or Codices of the New Testament. Where are they now? Describe each Codex.

Chapter V

23. Distinguish between a manuscript and a version.

24. What aspect of Alexander the Great's work contributed to the spread of the Scriptures?

25. What developments made it necessary to translate the Scriptures into other languages?

26. Describe the origin of the Septuagint Version of the Hebrew Scriptures.

27. What were the sources from which the Latin Vulgate was made?

Chapter VI

28. In what sense is the English Bible our heritage?

29. Describe the work of Caedmon. What is a paraphrase of the Scriptures?

30. What contribution did Bede make to the spread of the Scriptures among the Anglo-Saxon people?

31. What was the result of the Norman Conquest on English Bible translation?

Chapter VII

32. Name the factors that have greatly influenced the course of English Bible history from the Norman Conquest to the modern age.

33. Discuss the labors of William Tyndale. In what sense is Tyndale the father of our English Bible?

34. Describe the King James Version.

35. Give an estimate of the Revised Version.

CHAPTER VIII

36. Discuss the Bible in relation to mankind.

37. What is the relation of the Bible to our denominational beliefs and work? Name the five phases of our work which should always be seen in the light of the Bible.

38. What is the present attitude of students toward the new knowledge?

39. What is the special value of the Bible in the matter of life's goals and ideals?

40. In what way are students of today related to the future of the Bible and Bible study?